Wisdom as a Lifestyle

Wisdom as a Lifestyle

Building Biblical Life-Codes

David Wright

Lamplighter Books Grand Rapids, Michigan
Zondervan Publishing House

Wisdom as a Lifestyle
Copyright © 1987 by David Wright

Lamplighter Books is an imprint of Zondervan Publishing House,
1415 Lake Drive, S.E., Grand Rapids, Michigan 49506.

Library of Congress Cataloging in Publication Data

Wright, David (David W.)
  Wisdom as a lifestyle.

  Bibliography: p.
  1. Bible. O.T. Proverbs—Meditations. I. Title.
BS1465.4.W75   1986   242'.5   86-21083
ISBN 0-310-44311-3

Edited by Pamela M. Hartung

Printed in the United States of America

87 88 89 90 91 92 / EE / 10 9 8 7 6 5 4 3 2 1

CONTENTS

INTRODUCTION

It's been a long time since I've heard anyone complimented for being wise. The word "wise" often implies some degree of financial success ("So-and-so invested wisely") or a special sagacity far beyond the norm. But daily wisdom for life outside the marketplace seems outdated, having been replaced with wit, vision, energy, and persistence. Where and how does wisdom still apply to us?

Our culture surrounds us with a blinding array of possessions and technology. Everything we could ever wish for is at our fingertips and may be ours for a price. Almost any place on earth can be reached in a matter of hours; genetic engineering is no longer an unreachable goal; and our arsenals are filled with weapons whose destructive powers are beyond normal understanding. If satisfaction and security were to be found in possessions, in knowledge, or in defensive capabilities, we, of all people, should be most at ease.

But are we at ease? What do we have to cope with the life we have created? How do we choose our pleasures? How do we keep from being lonely? How can we resist being rendered superfluous by the machinery we have set in motion? In the silent hours when we must face life stripped of its glamor and activity, how do we face reality?

Life can be excruciatingly beautiful or disastrously ugly. We may find pleasure; we may find pain. Like it or not, we are forced to face life—to cope one way or another. Since we need guidelines to help direct us through life's maze, every one of us develops during his lifetime a code to sort and program the challenges. Although these codes may be subconscious, they are there.

A life-code is a controlling desire or motivator that produces values and rules for living, moving us to act in certain ways and value certain things. While a code may be shared, it is intensely personal and practical: how we treat our neighbors and why; how we spend our money and why; how we pass our time and why; or what character traits we value and seek to make our own. Drawing from our inherited personality traits, spiritual orientation, environment, training, and past experiences, our life-codes are, in a sense, our battle plans—ways we have decided to face life.

For several years, I've read the Book of Proverbs at least once a year and have been intrigued by the stability it pictures. Against its background, we see clear images of our frantic search for satisfaction: lonely people filling their lives with work or the latest technological toy; teens pasted to video screens; husbands and wives floating aimlessly, strangely, angrily through loves turned gray; church vestibule discussions that seldom rise higher than health, food, and fashion; the degrading erosion of self-esteem that plagues us; and the despair in facing temptations that always win.

In this book, I take an unconventional, and I hope refreshing, look at wisdom in Proverbs. Solomon teaches us that to the extent our life-codes fail to encompass our true nature as beings created in the image of God and dependent upon His grace, they will fail in the face of life's complexity. The root of our pain and fragmentation lies finally in our sinfulness—in our endless choices for ourselves against God. Yet even while we betray His love, He keeps holding it out to us.

God doesn't destroy His deserters. He gives them the warm intimacy of friendly conversation around crackling fires, the consuming pleasure of sexual relationships, the joy of shared love, and the awesome wonder of birth. He gives them a world of blue skies and gentle morning rain, deserts and high mountains, bird songs and lion roars. He gives them grace—the chance to start again—in hopes that someday they may see the futility of their foolish charade against the panoply of His majesty.

Wisdom as a Lifestyle bears the burden of showing not only how we struggle when we cling to life-codes that deny the outstretched hand of God but also how we may acknowledge Him by building the biblical life-code.

What life-code are you using? Is it working? Examine it and see whether you need to build the biblical life-code. Of all the other Old Testament characters, Solomon was the wisest. Through his example, we are shown how to build the life-code that will foster fulfillment and stability.

David Wright

1. Wisdom: The Biblical Life-Code

Every time they drove past the Rickerts' house on their way to prayer meeting, some remark would surface about the slovenly house, the raucous, dirty children in the yard, or the unmown grass littered with debris. They knew the name because it was proudly displayed on the mailbox at the end of the drive—The Rickert Residence.

Dan and Laurie could not understand why they seldom could think of anything else during prayer meeting except the Rickert family. Frankly, they were bothered. On an impulse, Laurie asked around and found that Mr. Rickert had been laid off for two years. Mrs. Rickert worked evenings at a local department store. They were not just poor but perilously close to being poor-and-hopelessly-so.

Late one Wednesday night, Dan and Laurie talked, wondering if God were prompting them to help the Rickerts in some way. Their favorite college professor, from whom they had learned the most about serving Christ, had often urged them to reach out to the needy. They recalled Dr. Romaine's lectures clearly even now: Christ doesn't really live in you until He lives out of you.

But when they thought of the ramifications of getting involved with the Rickerts—the riotous children plowing into their own neat little yard, the differences in their interests, the lack of any common ground on which to approach this family—they cringed.

Not long afterward, Laurie baked a loaf of bread and on the way to church one Wednesday night, Dan hurried up the walk to the Rickerts' door. The children stopped their playing to stare at this alien on their turf. Mr. Rickert seemed bewildered at first, then faintly gruff when he saw why Dan was there. Dan shoved the bread into his hands, mumbled a few words, and raced back to his car.

They figured they had tried. From then on, they rode past the Rickerts' house silently. They tried their best to enjoy prayer meeting, to ignore the feeling that God wasn't letting them off the hook yet.

· ● · ·

Climbing the executive ladder intrigued Jason. Even in childhood, he had had a knack for business. Later in business school, he had honed his methods of planning each advance. Each year he laid out his strategy, which seldom miscarried. He used any advantage that fell his way, yet somehow he retained a personable, dedicated demeanor. His co-workers liked him; his rivals respected him; and his immediate superiors eyed him nervously.

Jason was doubly disdainful of Rod's error. First, anyone with a modicum of business sense should have foreseen that the diversification for which Rod had fought could lead nowhere. Second, Rod had neglected to cover adequately the tracks of the corporate sleight of hand he had employed to pull the deal through. It had taken little effort on Jason's part to discover Rod's new vulnerabilities. He felt sure that when the time came, his knowledge of these weaknesses would lead to another step up.

Why had Carrie objected when he told her? he asked himself. Anyone as clumsy as Rod actually deserved to be shoved aside. What did some misguided sense of morality have in common with the real world of business?

• • ● • •

For what seemed the hundredth time, Shari pushed Joe's image from her mind, trying again to let the mellow music, the candlelight, and Rafe's interesting conversation chase away the lingering doubts. Was she right in being here? She knew where the evening was leading.

Through their three years together at Mason and Johnsons, their friendship had been constant. Always the gentleman, Rafe had let Shari know in subtle, pleasing ways that he found her attractive, and if she wished to accept his attention, he was ready to give it. He knew she was married, so he hadn't pushed.

At first, Shari had been careful to keep their friendship strictly that—a friendship. She liked Rafe's self-possessed and courtly manner, but she knew she loved Joe. She knew the perimeters of acceptable conduct. For her, it seemed simple until she discovered Joe's *mistake*. So much pain and anger seethed in her that even after they had patched things together, something in their relationship died. It grew easier, then, to let the distance creep between them, to let careers dictate their relationship. Over the last six months, the boundaries that had defined her friendship with Rafe had somehow crumbled. Although she was not in love with Rafe, he gave her what Joe had stopped giving her—attention. Shari found she liked it, and so she knew where this pleasant evening would end.

Why did she feel uneasy? Was she right or wrong? Was there *any* right or wrong in this situation?

LIFE AND LIFE-CODES

Dan and Laurie, Jason, and Shari are all immersed in the choice-forcing, often confusing mainstream of life. They are attempting to deal as best they can with the issues life has given them. How they respond to their circumstances will make their lives more vigorous and stable or more tangled and bruised. How will they know what will give them long-lasting satisfaction? How will they decide the best course to follow?

How would *you* or *I* decide? If you were in Shari's place, how would you choose your course? If you were Jason, would you take advantage of a ready-made opportunity to advance your career? In Dan and Laurie's shoes, would you reach out or withdraw?

Proverbs clarifies these kinds of questions. All of us choose criteria that become the basis of all other actions and choices throughout life. Sometimes our set of criteria is chosen consciously, as in Jason's case. When he decided to conquer the business world, his life's choices were oriented around that goal. But often these criteria are chosen unconsciously as the product of peer pressure and circumstances.

I have termed this set of criteria that serves as a basis for life's choices a life-code. Let's discover what happens when we try to live according to inadequate life-codes and how these produce frustration and broken lives. In contrast, an alternative called *wisdom* is taught in Proverbs, where the reader is encouraged to build biblical life-codes that will produce a radiancy and a contentment not often enjoyed these days.

WISDOM: THE BIBLICAL LIFE-CODE

Wisdom involves a special relationship with God, the One who alone can define and give life meaning. This life-code provides an equilibrium that steadies the soul and helps steer a true course through the bewildering maze life presents.

Wisdom teaches us who we are and gives us an inner landscape of fidelity to that knowledge. Through wisdom we learn how to give and to draw strength from our personal relationships as well as how to handle wealth or the lack of it. Wisdom even has its impact on our choice of words. Infusing our lives with freshness and vigor, it touches every aspect of our being.

In Proverbs 1, Solomon says the proverbs are given so that we may

> *know wisdom and instruction, discern the sayings of understanding, receive instruction in wise behaviour, righteousness, justice, and equity (vv. 2–3).[1]*

Although these words may sound archaic to our television-tuned ears, as we explore them, they will come alive and have special significance. Wise behavior, righteousness, justice, and equity are not dusty anachronisms but beacons of truth from which our lives need to take direction in the complexity of twentieth-century living.

Let's take a look at three of wisdom's most basic elements.

Wisdom Is Being in Touch with Reality

A common problem for those who labor under faulty life-codes is a failure to reckon with a fundamental reality about themselves.

Shari is almost ready to make a decision without taking this reality into consideration. Jason seems to have no clue that it even exists. And Dan and Laurie are in touch with it but they have not learned to walk in harmony with it. None of them have fully taken into account the existence of their souls, the spiritual dimension of their lives.

Wisdom's definition helps us to understand what Solomon was telling us in Proverbs. Wisdom speaks of "ability, worldly wisdom, and of prudence." But in a general sense, wisdom is said to be "the knowledge of things in the essence of their being and in the reality of their existence."[2] Simply speaking, wisdom is learning who we are and what is required to make our existence on earth a productive and satisfying proposition—being in touch with the truths behind the visible world of bodies and possessions.[3] Proverbs does not promise Utopia. People living by biblical life-codes may suffer. However, what we gain through wisdom is a basic understanding of what sort of creatures we are, which clarifies a whole new way of life for us.

It is quite possible to go through life without really knowing who we are, why we are alive, or what we might do to make life more than a mere "scrape-by-and-get-what-you-can-on-the-way" existence. Trying to live this way is a guaranteed formula for fractured personhood and frustrated relationships.

As a life-code, wisdom's beauty lies in its teaching us the inner reality that directs our world and our lives—our relationship with God. We learn that He knows us even more fully than we can ever know ourselves and that, inexplicably, He loves us. This unlocks secrets about our lives we never knew. This wisdom gives us the courage to be ourselves (nothing else will) and helps us find our place in the community around us. We love because we know we are loved. We find ourselves trying to reach the real in others. We find keys to unlock the world's majesty and beauty because we know ourselves to be the products of God's vast love.

Wisdom Is Being Able to Make Sound Judgments

Solomon aimed to teach wisdom. As a corollary, he tried to help his hearers "discern the sayings of understanding" (1:2). One of the biblical life-code's basic elements is the ability to choose soundly when faced with life's intimidating array of alternatives. When Solomon speaks of understanding, he describes a special ability: "The right criteria [for] distinguishing between the true and the false, the good and the bad, the wholesome and the pernicious."[4] Wisdom includes having the tools to make sound judgments.

We are bombarded daily with persuasive arguments for all sorts of things. Our money, our time, our influence, and our sympathy are diligently solicited by those with things to sell, ideas to trade, or causes to push. Our life-code becomes the arbitrator of what we embrace or reject.

As a fixture of their life-code, Dan and Laurie love their own little world and are loathe to have it disturbed. So it is difficult for them to judge whether reaching out to the Rickerts would be a worthwhile endeavor because of their undue regard for the tried and true.

Using the biblical life-code, we learn to choose soundly, basing our choices on a clear-eyed appraisal of the true and trustworthy, not the false. Little by little, wisdom comes into us and into our daily circumstances. As we allow God to rebuild our approaches to life, we find useful, reassuring, dependable criteria on which to base our decisions. This is a remarkable, satisfying way to live!

Wisdom Is Being Uncompromisingly Honest

Wisdom includes another basic element—honesty.

—— When I was seven, my father taught me a lesson I have not forgotten. We lived on the campus of a Bible school on the Philippine Islands. Dad was the president of this school, and Mother taught several classes. During the day, my friends and I were free to roam the grounds picking guavas, playing with trucks, or riding our bikes.

Back on one corner of the campus were two typical Filipino family dwellings of split bamboo with heavy thatched roofs. Perfectly suited to the hot, humid climate, they were open and cool. Built on stilts, they were sturdy and practical. But they were also firetraps. One stray match could reduce the whole house to a gray mound of ash in a matter of minutes. Needless to say, no one played with fire in those homes—no one but Johnny and I. Though we had been warned, one day the temptation was too strong, and time was heavy on our hands. While everyone else was in class, we sneaked into one of those houses and tried to build a fire in the earthen kitchen stove.

After several minutes, we both began to feel uncomfortable. We had miraculously failed to burn the house down; nevertheless, we knew we were disobeying. Shortly, we spied someone coming down the lane to the house. Arms and legs went every direction as we tumbled out the back door. Cautiously, I made my way through the garden at the rear of our house until I came to the door and quietly let myself in.

Safe! I thought. When Dad got home, my nonchalance was conspicuous. Strangely, he began asking uncomfortably pointed questions. After a few minutes of this close questioning, my bravado crumbled and I confessed. The punishment was severe and effective. I learned two lessons that day: Never to play with fire in those houses and always to remain uncompromisingly honest even if truth is uncomfortable.

Shari had accepted a duty, not based simply on social mores but on the fundamental reality of the human soul. She had given her word to remain faithful to her husband. Although consistent with a life-code that urges us to take pleasure where it may be found, to be unfaithful would finally reduce her to a racked soul.

In Proverbs 1:3, Solomon says that the proverbs give us instruction about wise behavior. He clarified wise behavior to include righteousness, justice, and equity. When he placed these nouns in juxtaposition to wise behavior, Solomon suggested "a way of thought and of conduct that is straight, according to what is right, true, without concealment, honest, true to duty, and faithful to one's word."[5]

As a lifestyle, one of wisdom's central elements is a streak of this kind of honesty. Proverbs seeks to instill habits of mind that are without concealment, true to duty, and faithful to our word.

Values such as fidelity, honesty, sincerity, sometimes treated with an air of disdain, are indispensable for inner strength and tranquility. Anyone who lives by falsehood is doomed to a life of schizophrenic tension between what he is and what he has claimed to be. How much simpler to be true to ourselves and to our word.

• • ● • •

If Shari, Jason, Dan, and Laurie cling to life-codes formed on something other than the Word of God, they will not see that the lasting values—what makes for real satisfaction—are those that build honesty and integrity and are closest to the inner reality of their souls. Life's circumstances are where our inner lives are built and matured. Learning to live as God teaches, we find the only satisfaction that can last. Our ultimate goal is to learn to be like God as we learn biblical life-codes.

Long before she had come to grips with her tumbling thoughts, Shari had finished the last of her lime sherbet, and Rafe was laying his credit card into the check tray. *I refuse to spoil this evening,* she told herself firmly. In a few minutes, they were driving to Rafe's luxurious townhouse. Shari had to admit that she had enjoyed the pleasant meal, the interesting conversation, and Rafe's constant, kind attention. She felt the last of the long-held, seldom-questioned system of dos and don'ts silently slip away. *It was a relic from childhood anyway,* she reasoned to herself. *After all, this is the twentieth century, and it isn't as though I don't have some right to my own happiness.*

Sadly, what Shari thinks is an adequate basis for dealing with life-choices actually is a less-than-adequate substitute for wisdom.

2. What Wisdom Isn't

When Shari decided to take advantage of what appeared to be a promising opportunity for happiness, she was using a life-code that didn't give her all the information she needed to make her choice. She sensed only a vague warning that she would be more dissatisfied than before. That warning seemed to be rooted in a code of values inherited from an earlier, less complicated era—a code to which she felt little attachment. When it came to the point of choosing, Shari acted on the basis of an inadequate life-code.

LIFE-CODES THAT FAIL

A life-code is an overarching structure of ideas and values we use to govern our lives. The more consistently we build this life-code according to God's wisdom, the better are our chances of leading lives of peace and inner joy. All life-codes fall short if they are not built on biblical principles. This is the burden of Proverbs, where we receive the instructions we need to build life-codes reflecting biblical principles.

Wisdom is learned over the course of our lives as we put into practice the truths of God's Word. If we take the trouble to examine ourselves, we may find in ourselves a habit of approaching life that falls short of wisdom. There are three kinds of life-codes that may *resemble* wisdom but actually are far inferior to it.

Shari had learned a code of moral, emotional, and physical values from her family heritage. It worked for her until it came under pressure, then it failed. An inherited value system is not wisdom.

Jason believed strongly in himself and his ability to analyze life's opportunities. He felt he could make all of life respond to the few cardinal rules he had learned in childhood and later perfected in business school: Plan well; work hard; take the breaks; consolidate the gains; then reap the rewards. This sort of rote approach to life is not wisdom.

Dan and Laurie came the closest to living according to a biblical life-code. In fact, many elements were already present. Their contact with their college professor had taught them much about what it meant to live by the dictates of God's Word; however, they had not gotten beyond the stage of seeking to emulate their teacher's role. The Word of God had not permeated their lives directly to spread out into all their protected corners. Simply imitating role models is not wisdom.

Let's take a closer look at these three substitutes for a biblical life-code.[1]

Inherited Values

In a course I once took, the teacher related an interesting experience. During the course of their marriage, he and his wife began to notice that a misunderstanding, perhaps over some kitchen procedure, was producing an undue amount of friction. After some time of wrestling with the problem and finding no solution, my professor decided to bring the issue to a head. After a particularly trying argument, he asked his wife, "Why must we do it that way instead of any other way?" After reflecting, she responded with some surprise, "Well I guess because that's the way my mother did it." He said, "Isn't that funny. My mother did it just the opposite way." By tracing their actions back to their roots, they discovered the basic difference that had caused the friction and were able to move closer to a solution.

We would probably be surprised if we knew how much of our value systems is inherited from our childhood. Although we might be tempted to believe we live in an age where there is no such thing as an inherited value system, this is not true. Even though traditional values have long since come under intense fire and in many cases have disappeared, we do not live and are incapable of living in a moral vacuum. Values are being handed down whether we recognize them or not.

The problem with inherited value codes is that they are not really our own but are a part of the cultural, perhaps emotional, baggage we use to travel through life. Thus, they are simply circumstances of our lives. If we happen to inherit a code of values that has some resemblance to biblical truth, we are fortunate. But sometimes we are not so fortunate. When an opposing wind begins to blow on our unexamined superstructure of values, as in Shari's case, it is likely to crash.

Many lose their way when confronted with the stark alternatives of the world because their code of values is inherited, unchosen, and without purpose or reason. Without a volitional, reasoned foundation, these value codes collapse like a house of cards in the storm of ideas raging in today's world. Simply to inherit a code of values is not wisdom.

The Rote Approach

Everyone's heard of Pavlov's dogs. Ring a bell, then give a dog a piece of meat day after day, month after month, and he will begin to put two and two together. Dogs aren't stupid. They soon learn bell equals meat.

That kind of rote training is a most effective way to teach certain things to people. My one-year-old daughter knows very well which shelf of books is off-limits. When she touches it, she hears a stern No. If she continues, we may punish her. It doesn't take her long to put two and two together. She has learned that she cannot play with those books.

Something that is learned by rote is done mechanically without any understanding of the whys and wherefores of the action.[2] When applied to the formation and use of a life-code, it translates into a structured but shallow approach to life.

There are those, like our fictional Jason, who have had ingrained in themselves a set of rules to face life. Life is tested against these rules, and what doesn't fit is thrown aside—to be ignored or neglected.

For example, Jason felt that if he planned, worked hard, achieved, and then reaped the benefits of this effort, his life would be meaningful. His life-code did not include the fact that planning and hard work don't always produce what we expect. Achieving does not, in itself, produce peace. Such things as charity, hope, and personal relationships cannot be so quantified and manipulated.

Almost mechanically, Jason was fulfilling the dictates of his cardinal rules. When they fail to produce, he will redouble his efforts, thinking he has planned wrong, neglected to work hard enough, or allowed a gap in the structure. When he still finds peace and meaning elusive, he will be at a loss.

I have used Jason as an example, but it is not only achievers like him who live by a rote life-code. The principle of the rote approach—learn a fixed set of values and then force life to fit these rules—can be used by those of a religious bent to decide moral issues. Every moral question may be forced into black-and-white categories until the minutia of life are covered by endless laws all carrying the same weight. This was the system of the Pharisees.

Unfortunately, such rote systems do not wear well as life-codes because they lack flexibility to handle the complexity of life. A life-code must be dynamic and, by its nature, consist of overarching principles that are free to find expression according to the circumstances that bring them into play. Attempting to memorize a few stock answers and forcing life to fit those answers is not the way of wisdom.

Imitating Role Models

Imitating role models isn't all bad; it's practically unavoidable. All of us at some time need someone who will give us a standard to aim for. Although most frequently when we are young, even as adults we admire and learn from certain individuals.

One of my most powerful role models was a college Bible teacher. For a long time, I held little respect for him because his values were so different from mine when I was a crusader for righteous causes. I judged him as something less than a "mature" Christian. However, I still had to take his classes. Day after day, I sat in class grudgingly admiring his astute grasp of the Word. He obviously enjoyed Bible study, and his enthusiasm was contagious. But I stubbornly refused to allow myself to respect him.

Then one day he taught a lesson on the redemptive love of God. He told us how his little daughter had almost been killed by a car and the anguish he had felt. Tearfully he related his experience to the love that God must have had for us to send His only Son to die for us. For the first time, I saw how deeply he loved the Lord I was serving so self-righteously. That day my prejudice was broken, and I was able to love and respect him. He became the one college and seminary professor to have the most influence on my life.

While we may gain a great deal from the imitation of such role models, real dangers are inherent. Uncritical, nondiscerning acceptance of people will betray us in three ways. First, no human is perfect. If we are not careful, we will imitate the flaws of our heroes, along with their strengths. Second, all humans will fall short of our expectations at some point. The subsequent disillusionment may tarnish all the good they might have taught us. Third, as Dan and Laurie found, if our life-code is molded by our attempts to build on the model of another's life instead of the Word of God, we will be incomplete. While some elements may well be exemplary, others may be far from acceptable.

LEARNING THE LIFE-CODES THAT SUCCEED

Each of these methods fails to teach us wisdom. Inherited codes of value fail because they have no basis in a willful, intelligent choice on our part. Rote training fails because it is unable to recognize and deal with life's complexity. Simply imitating role models fails because it makes fallible humans our standard.

What we must have in place of these is a pervasive, inclusive, volitional knowledge of the whys and wherefores of life.[3] We must not simply know what values we hold, we must know why we hold them. Our life-code must be truly our own, be flexible enough to give us the tools to meet life realistically, and ultimately, have its roots in the principles of God's Word.

How do we develop this sort of life-code? According to Proverbs, if we wish to learn wisdom, we must do so by a twofold process. First, we must build an intimate relationship with God because wisdom is a product of such a relationship. Proverbs 1:7 serves as a motto for the entire book, "The fear of the Lord is the beginning of knowledge [or wisdom]." It is the school where we learn.

Second, wisdom is a product of a lifelong process of character building. Each circumstance of life has something to teach us about wisdom. As we walk with God, He teaches us through the years. By solving daily problems with the tools He gives, we learn more about wisdom.

We are assured in Proverbs that "wisdom comes from God, and whoever fears Him receives it."[4] Centuries later, James wrote, "If any of you lacks wisdom, he should ask God, who gives generously to all without finding fault, and it will be given to him" (James 1:5, NIV).[5] To fear God is to acknowledge Him as Master of the universe—our Creator and Sustainer—and to acknowledge His right to be Himself and exercise His prior claim upon our lives. In the face of His power and love, we say, "I renounce my imposter's role as lord of my life and yield the throne room to You who created it for Yourself." Here is the beginning of wisdom. Until we renounce ourselves, our whole existence is built on a debilitating falsehood that mars everything we think and all we do. When we acknowledge the lordship of God, we build a firm foundation that abolishes this fundamental struggle of human life. Wisdom will grow only in this climate, on this foundation.

How do we pursue wisdom? We must accept an apparent contradiction: If you want really to own something, first let go of it. Here is the paradox in learning wisdom. Although wisdom promises us a life of satisfaction, offering a measure of health, perhaps even of wealth, not available by any other means, if we say, "I want health and wealth so I will strike off after wisdom," we will never reach any of the three—health, wealth, or wisdom.

We must understand that if we pursue wisdom *to be happy and wealthy,* we will never find it. If we pursue wisdom because it offers a life of devotion to God, we will find peace of mind, fulfillment, and true joy along the way. As we learn from reading C. S. Lewis, we don't serve God because He is good to us but because He is God. We aren't Christians because Christianity is nice but because it is true.

Wisdom, we are told, calls us. Like an imploring lover, she seeks us out. And just as any lover may be repulsed by a spirit of exploitation in her beloved, Wisdom will not yield her treasures to anyone who says, "Let me catch her to take her charms of wealth and health and peace of mind."

If we lend a willing ear and learn, we benefit. If we turn a deaf ear, we lose. In chapter three, we will see what happens when we cause Wisdom to withdraw either by inattentiveness or slowness of heart—when we are left to make do with some faulty life-code.

3. When Wisdom Withdraws

I have had no firsthand experience of war. Whether the rationale used to train troops holds true, I cannot say. Often, in times of great confusion and stress when we are under attack, our actions are more or less limited to instinctive behavior. I do know this principle seems to prove itself in other areas of life.

In the mad melee of battle with hot lead singeing our ears, we have difficulty thinking logically, thoughtfully weighing the relative merits of several courses of action. Instead we act quickly in the ways we have been trained. Generally speaking, the old adage "He who hesitates is lost" is particularly apropos to the man in battle.

For this reason, when a man enlists as a soldier, he spends countless hours in basic training designed to make instinctive the actions required of him in battle. He learns to use his weapons under all conditions. He learns unquestioning obedience to his commanding officers. He trains physically until his body is lean and strong. All of this so, ideally, under attack he won't stand arguing with his officers, forget which is the business end of his gun, or collapse breathlessly at the feet of his enemy.

To change our analogy, we find the same principles holding true in sports. Success always depends on being able to do the little things well without having to think about them. When a good manager is asked to turn a cellar-dwelling baseball team into world champions, he begins with the fundamentals. He knows the double plays, the shutouts, the big innings come only after his players have mastered the basic building blocks of throwing, catching, and playing as a team. Flawless play under pressure is a product of hours and hours of practice, so the required actions have become second nature.

Likewise if we want wisdom to see us through the battles of our lives, we must be learning the fundamentals before the battles arrive. Crises are not the time to go looking for wisdom. What we have been building into our character day by day is what we will use under pressure. If we have been applying ourselves to the lessons each day sets before us to learn wisdom, we will reap the harvest when the crises come.

Solomon gives us a graphic account of what happens when Wisdom is ignored.

> *Wisdom shouts in the street,*
> *She lifts her voice in the square;*
>
> *At the head of the noisy streets she cries out;*
> *At the entrance of the gates in the city, she*
> *   utters her sayings:*
>
> *"How long, O naive ones, will you love simplicity?*
> *And scoffers delight themselves in scoffing,*
> *And fools hate knowledge?*
>
> *"Turn to my reproof,*
> *Behold, I will pour out my spirit on you;*
> *I will make my words known to you.*
>
> *"Because I called, and you refused;*
> *I stretched out my hand, and no one paid attention;*
>
> *"And you neglected all my counsel,*
> *And did not want my reproof;*
>
> *"I will even laugh at your calamity;*
> *I will mock when your dread comes,*

> *"When your dread comes like a storm,*
> *And your calamity comes on like a whirlwind,*
> *When distress and anguish come on you.*
>
> *"Then they will call on me, but I will not answer;*
> *They will seek me diligently, but they shall not find me,*
>
> *"Because they hated knowledge,*
> *And did not choose the fear of the Lord.*
>
> *"They would not accept my counsel,*
> *They spurned all my reproof.*
>
> *"So shall they eat of the fruit of their own way,*
> *And be satiated with their own devices.*
>
> *"For the waywardness of the naive shall kill them,*
> *And the complacency of fools shall destroy them.*
>
> *"But he who listens to me shall live securely,*
> *And shall be at ease from the dread of evil"(1:20–33).*

We have talked about our pursuit of wisdom but here we learn Wisdom pursues us even when we aren't looking for her. Issuing an invitation to all who will listen, she is like a lady who calls people to receive her gifts. Unfortunately, she is often ignored. Those who turn away face grave consequences. Because they have not learned wisdom as a soldier learns to fight or an athlete learns to play, they are defeated even before they begin.

WISDOM'S INVITATION

Something makes a secret fascinating. What is hidden we long to uncover. We are forever beguiled by what lies just beyond the next range of mountains. Even a closed door holds a silent attraction few can resist.

In religion, the attraction of the mysterious has always been a powerful force. History is strewn with teachers who have claimed some secret initiation into life's inner circles. The meaning of existence has been sought in many mystical Valhallas, their entrances described to awe-struck disciples by revered professors-of-the-way. Almost without exception, they have claimed to possess some special key to unlock the riddles that have plagued people's minds since time began. There has always been some piece of knowledge, some liberating experience, or some holy act known only to a few, however, available at a price.

Even the Christian church has had its share of those who have claimed a "special" relationship with God, gained through some esoteric experience. Some inner enlightenment or asceticism has been required to move from the fringes of God's presence into His throne room.

While most "keys to better living" have been offered as hidden and mysterious things, wisdom is portrayed in just the opposite way. In Solomon's words, "Wisdom calls aloud in the street, she raises her voice in the public squares; at the head of the noisy streets she cries out, in the gateways of the city she makes her speech" (1:20–21, NIV). Far from being hidden, Wisdom is available in the most public places. Instead of being reticent, Wisdom is bold; instead of being retiring, she is forthright. She thrusts herself into the mainstream of life saying, "Here I am. Please listen to me."

It is not truth that is hard to find. If we want life bursting with springlike freshness, rooted in the equilibrium of eternity, it is ours for the taking. But our eyes are blind, and our ears dull. Forever in search of that final elusive bit of satisfaction, we race down a thousand dead-end lanes, hoping to find the Subject our souls were made to crave in the objects of our lives. Sometimes chuckling, sometimes weeping, but always watching, always waiting, always wooing, He pursues us all the while. And if we stop to listen in the stillness of our evacuated hearts, we will hear the unmistakable voice of home.

Wisdom is the way of life produced by a relationship with God. It is not a hidden life or a life hard to understand. If we take the necessary steps of repentance and faith, we may enter an existence where God will mark the further steps we must take. Daily He will teach us more about

Himself and about the kind of life that will bring us peace and Him glory. If we have already asked Jesus to be our Savior and yet find our lives full of tension, frustration, anger, and disillusionment, we have not really made Him our Lord in a practical, specific way. We need to settle concretely the issue of whose leadership we will follow— God's or our own. Then we will need to make every effort to bend our spiritual ears in His direction, seeking His will in all matters and following it diligently.

Just as the mysterious has held an attraction for people who have wanted to learn truth, isolation has often seemed the best way to learn God's ways. Although wisdom is learned by daily obedience to God's will, quite often we meet those who say if we really want to be like God—to know His ways—we must insulate ourselves from the evil around us. We must take ourselves out of the arenas where men who don't follow truth have their way. Since we live in a world of ungodly men, we must take care not to mix with them or to take on their ways.

As Christians, we are given new lives, ones radically different from our friends who don't know our Lord. But why should we want to imitate the lives of people who don't follow God when we have found something as delightful as following Christ? Still, Proverbs tells us, "Wisdom raises her voice in the public squares; at the head of the noisy streets she cries out, in the gateways of the city she makes her speech." Every day in the noisy stream of life, Wisdom calls people to herself. Since all kinds of competing voices are heard, we may not hear her. But she is there, battling to be heard, too. If we really want to learn wisdom, we must plunge into life with every ounce of energy we possess. God has given us a beautiful world, yet full of problems, hunger, and hurt—full of chances to learn His way with people.

Wisdom is in the rush of the day and in the rising stillness of the night. Her call is a fading whisper in the voice of the man you hate and a song in the one you love.

She is even in the ancient eyes of old men who anchor their park benches like bookends.[1] She laughs in the voices of children and pleads in the gaping eyes of wired youth. She speaks from every experience, every occasion, every individual we meet. Her invitation is everywhere, "Turn to my reproof, behold, I will pour out my spirit on you; I will make my words known to you" (1:23).

WISDOM'S AUDIENCE

As Wisdom's invitation floats out among the many competing voices of the world, there is no assurance that it will find lodging in open, hungry hearts. From Wisdom's speech in chapter one, we see the chances are great that her message will be lost in the wind. She says, "How long, O naive ones, will you love simplicity? And scoffers delight themselves in scoffing, and fools hate knowledge?"(1:22).

When I was a beginning flight student, I learned an interesting lesson on the value of listening. I had only about a dozen hours of flight time completed, but my instructor judged me competent to practice takeoffs and landings by myself.

For a student, cross-wind landings are the most difficult, since the wind blows across rather than down the runway. Pilots spend much time learning to master the tricky technique of putting the airplane on the runway as opposed to the field alongside it. One day I was practicing in a stiff Indiana cross wind. All of my concentration was required to land without breaking off the wheels sideways underneath me. As usual, I listened to the traffic on the radio and made regular reports of my position. After a while, I decided to start around for my last landing. I heard another pilot report that he was five miles away, coming in to land. *Five miles? No sweat. I'll be taxiing back to the hangar by the time he gets here,* I thought.

I had neglected to consider two things: the kind of

plane he was flying and the runway he would be landing on. He was flying a Learjet, which could run circles around little trainers like mine, and since his jet couldn't land on the short runway I was using, he would land on the long one that crossed mine.

Unconcerned, I trundled on around toward my runway. Seeing the developing situation, my instructor called me repeatedly to tell me to go a little farther out before landing to give the jet time to land and clear the runways. I ignored him. I was so preoccupied with doing everything right for my landing that I didn't even see the jet until it passed in front of me at the intersection.

Similarly, our lives are often so filled with other interests that we find it easy to ignore Wisdom's invitations. Because we do not listen, we do not learn. Our denials come in different ways. In chapter one, Wisdom talks to three kinds of people who reject her. They are "the simple, the mockers, and the fools,"[2]—three responses to the life-code God recommends.

The Simple

The first response is an interesting one. The lives of the simple are like fields of corn without fences, which stand open to anyone and anything that wishes to trample across them. Their hearts are susceptible to every passing influence, so anything offering a flashing lure will attract their attention. The simple are easy prey for all the latest fads, whether spiritual, philosophical, or social, because they seldom question the influences pushing them here and there. They are content simply to drift with the shifting tides of life.

There may well be a certain harmless good-naturedness about these folks, who do not threaten those around them and can always be counted on to follow the crowd. But they will never contribute much to life. They fall prey to the winds, having no conviction to say, "This is who I am." Consequently, they cannot, or will not, chart and follow a purposeful course through life. Rather, they naively pin their fate on each successive fantasy.

When Wisdom's invitation comes to these people, it comes simply as another attraction. Wisdom cannot make any real inroads into their character or affections because Wisdom demands purpose and commitment. Not being a fad, wisdom is lost to the simple.

We should ask ourselves from time to time, *Who am I? Where is my life going? Am I simply drifting or am I living purposefully and coherently?* If we find ourselves coasting on the tailwinds of life, we need to stop and make some deep commitments to learn wisdom and let God inject some backbone into our lives

The Mockers

The second response is the mocker's—the scoffer's. Intellectual honesty is a virtue we hold in high esteem. We demand reasons to believe, and we try not to believe except for reasons that merit faith. But with this virtue comes a parallel fault. We may find it easy to hide our rebellion against God's way behind the pretense of honest doubt.

I think a crippling malaise of our culture is its pervasive skepticism of anything metaphysical. From their earliest years in school, children imbibe a mindset that leaves no room for objective knowledge except in the realm of science. Yet we are told that nothing in the area of morality or values is universal. All is relative—untrue at some point or for some person. To fix life on certain immovable morals has become a foreign mode of thought. One of the most difficult struggles in my Christian life has been overcoming this subconscious resistance to universally binding truth. I don't think I am alone.

Here in Proverbs we run straight into the notion that those who are scoffers close themselves off from truth. What is the relationship between the prevalent mindset I have described and Proverbs' scoffer?

Solomon speaks of the scoffer as someone who insists on questioning everything, not from the motive of honest inquiry but from his own rebellion. He does not wish to arrive at truth but to obscure it, so he can escape the responsibility it brings.

My concern is that we, in our present condition, may fail to respond positively to Wisdom's invitation through two errors. We may be so jaded intellectually and spiritually that we simply will not give credence to Wisdom's call. Or, we may cling so strongly to our cherished right of freethinking, we will refuse to acknowledge the truth of Wisdom's claims. By stubbornly maintaining "We will not be duped," we miss our chances to know truth.

I was once acquainted with a fellow who could have fit Solomon's description of a scoffer. I'll call him Ron. Ron and I became friends when we worked side by side on the night shift at our lumber mill. Ron came from back East and had migrated, for various reasons of his own, to the Northwest. He was a child of the sixties, having come through the turbulent years when the Vietnam debacle threatened to rip our country apart. I recall his telling me how he saw national guardsmen charge across the commons where he had played as a boy, weapons ready, intent on dispersing demonstrators. Ron was bitter. He cherished his freedom from constraint and was unceasingly cynical of government, the church, and even those of us he worked with. He, however, was personable. Ron was his own man, albeit without inner peace.

Many nights Ron and I talked during equipment breakdowns. While the millwrights worked, we discussed everything from the war to politics in general, to religion, to personal tastes. In these verbal sparring sessions, Ron was intelligent and educated enough to ask probing questions. When we spoke of faith in Christ, he was interested but, again, cynical. Night after night we talked, and day after day I prayed for Ron. Finally, I gave him C. S. Lewis's *Mere Christianity,* a small volume but one that had helped me immensely in my grappling with faith. I hoped it might give us further material for discussion.

After reading it, Ron was angry. He told me clearly that he did not think any book could convert him, least of all this one. I agreed. He poured out his bitterness and his anger, and I saw something that I had felt but not yet known definitely. Ron was one of Solomon's scoffers: He probed with his mind, but he had closed his heart to truth. Even though he defended his right to be free from constraint, he steadfastly refused to see how his own will held him bondage. He did not wish to face the painful dilemma of acting on the Truth, which came stealing into his life.

Solomon tells us clearly that a time comes when our false intellectual skepticism must be seen for the evasive tactic it is. If we wish to learn wisdom, we must come to learn, not to fight.

The Fools

The word "fool" has all but lost its meaning through its usage in our language. Nevertheless, let's look at several clues to help us see the fools' response to wisdom. First, Wisdom says, "How long will fools hate knowledge?" Unlike common usage, a fool is not simply one who forgets, but one who actually hates knowledge—who does not want to learn. He is content in his ways and has no interest in being jolted from them.

Looking further, we find the word translated here as "fool" comes from an Arabic word that means "to be thick, coarse, indolent."[3] Therefore, a fool is one who, either by birth or by habit, is impervious to the message of truth. If our natural condition predisposes us to such a state, God's grace will undoubtedly keep us. Much more often, though, we render ourselves foolish.

During World War II, it was necessary for submarines to run a certain amount of time on the surface. Watchmen in the conning tower kept a lookout for other vessels. Out on the ocean, where all was dark, good night vision was a must. Before going on watch, the sailors sat in a room lit only by dim red lights. After going on watch, it would still take many minutes before their eyes were fully adjusted. Their eyes needed to acquire acute sensitivity to catch the faintest glimmer of light in the darkness.

Proverbs' fools have blinded themselves to truth by filling their spiritual vision with the garish glow of the world's imitations. Their senses are dulled by all the worldly trash in their lives. Sensuality, gluttonous consumption of wholesome things, and constant resistance to God's voice make us deeply insensitive to spiritual truth. As a result, we hate knowledge with a genuine hatred because we have become mental and spiritual imbeciles.

If we wish to respond to Wisdom's invitation, we must protect our sensitivity to spiritual truth. Our lives should be filled with healthy, balanced wholesome influences. We need to cultivate our spiritual senses daily so we can see the true light among the glittering reflections about us.

When Wisdom Withdraws

What are the consequences of failing to respond to Wisdom's invitation? What is God's response to our rebellion and Wisdom's response to our refusals? In this life, God responds as a father whose love never ends. Regardless of how often or how deep our rebellion, He will welcome us home with open arms if we choose to return. Jesus' parable of the prodigal son is a touching example. God is like the anxious father who kept an eye on the long, dusty road for his rebellious son. His constant hope was to see that son coming home. Finally, one marvelous day it happened. In the distance, he saw a familiar figure stumbling up the road, broken and defeated. His heart bursting with joy, the father spared no expense to welcome and restore his prodigal son. God waits to welcome us back, too.

Wisdom's response to our refusals is different. Wisdom is not God, but a way of life. God uses circumstances to teach us this way of life. But if we continually refuse to be taught, though He loves us and wishes we would learn, He will not force us. All He can do is abandon us to the ways we have chosen. Wisdom appears as a beneficent friend whose advances, often spurned, are finally withdrawn. All of the gifts she wishes to give are forfeited. Even though we will want her gifts someday, then she will not, cannot give them. Wisdom must be welcomed into our lives daily. When crises come, wisdom will carry us through if we have allowed her to teach us daily lessons. But she will not be called in as a means of rescue just to be abandoned as soon as the crisis is past.

In Proverbs 1:24–25, Wisdom accuses those who refuse her gifts. Like a deeply wounded friend, she details her indictment.

I called . . . You refused.
I stretched out my hands . . . You didn't pay attention.
I offered counsel . . . You neglected.
I offered reproof . . . You didn't want it.

Then in verses 29 and 30 (paraphrased), she outlines the responses of those she has invited but who have refused her invitations. In their answers, she shows them what they are really like.

You hated knowledge.
You did not choose to fear the Lord.
You would not accept my counsel.
You spurned all my reproof.

Life is full of chances to learn the life-code God recommends. If we spurn them, our refusals will snowball until when we need help, we have nothing and no one to turn to. The normal struggles of marriage relationships increase until, not having trained ourselves in God's strength, divorce inundates us. Financial drains, family tensions, career crises, temptations, when faced without the help of God's wisdom, become insurmountable obstacles. We are broken like a fragile ship dashed by the storms against a rocky coast because we have lost our lighthouse.

Psalm 107:10–11 says, "There were those who dwelt in darkness and in the shadow of death, prisoners in misery and chains, *because* they had rebelled against the words of God, and spurned the counsel of the Most High." To spurn something means to reject it as unworthy of our interest. Thus, spurning God's counsel is an expression of our inner rebellion. Even when we are careless toward God, we spurn Him because we deny the importance of His counsel by not being careful to keep it. If we have been practicing a life full of wrong priorities, when we most need His wisdom, we will not find it. Wisdom is gained through experience, diligence, and obedience, not at a moment's notice.

Having outlined her indictment, Wisdom announces its consequences by relating three struggles we will face alone in verses 26 through 28 (paraphrased).

> *(1) When your calamity comes like a whirlwind, I will laugh.*
>
> *(2) When your dread comes like a storm, I will mock.*
>
> *(3) When your distress and anguish come, you will call, but I will not answer.*

Wisdom details vividly some of the most frequent and feared occurrences of our lives. *Calamity* is that sudden, unannounced devastation, which haunts our secret thoughts. Though we may spend a lifetime building a livelihood, we fear it can be destroyed in one year of recession. Or, in our moments of greatest joy, we feel that nagging strain of fear that our fortune is too good to last. In the twinkling of an eye, those we love most may be taken from us. Nothing in this life is permanent, least of all happiness. Then, Wisdom will say, "When all you cherish is wiped out by some sudden destruction, though I could have been there to give you some solidity to cling to, because you spurned me, all I can do is laugh at the irony of your failure."

Dread is a heavy sense of foreboding, the approaching storm that sometimes grips our minds and hearts. It is the paralyzing fear of those things just beyond our consciousness, always vaguely threatening. For a generation, the world has lived in dread of a nuclear holocaust. The fear of it is imbedded in our subconscious. There it becomes not simply an awful possibility but a mounting probability. "Someday," Fear says, "someday . . ." And Wisdom says, "When all of life is graying with your dread, though I could have been there to give you hope, because you spurned me, my strength can only mock your stormy failure."

Distress is an endless dreary march of vexing circumstances, which taxes our strength and drains our patience. *Anguish* is the half-born fear that squeezes joy and peace from our lives. Together these can produce an endless, dispirited exhaustion, so we face each day defeated before the grinding demands of daily life. Our zest of spirit, the spring in our step, and the laugh in our voice are all lost. Then, Wisdom says, "When life looks like an endlessly black horizon, though I could have been there to give you the glory of dawn's breaking, because you spurned me, my rays of joy will only echo in the dismal chambers of your night teaching you the extent of your sad failure."

Proverbs paints bleak pictures for those who choose to ignore Wisdom's invitation. If we ignore her, not all of life will be barren and ugly, but a joy and strength will be missing. At some crucial crossroads when the rest of life depends on our decision, we will not have the resources to choose wisely. "The waywardness of the naive shall kill them, and the complacency of fools shall destroy them" (1:32).

If, on the other hand, we accept Wisdom's invitation, we welcome into every aspect of our lives a healthy invigorating freshness. Everything will not be rosy, but we will have help to face life's perplexing problems. Then, we have Wisdom's promise, "He who listens to me shall live securely, and shall be at ease from the dread of evil" (1:33).

· • ● • ·

We face much bleakness when we try to live by faulty life-codes. Treasures await us, however, when we follow the biblical life-code!

4. Wisdom's Structures

There are consequences for ignoring wisdom, and the pictures painted in Proverbs aren't encouraging. Fortunately, there is a bright side, too. Although wisdom ignored results in frustration and brokenness, wisdom welcomed brings health and equilibrium.

SPHERES OF EXPERIENCE

Silicon Valley is light years behind the human personality. Nothing is so intricate, so awesome as the psyche of man. Only someone wholly above and beyond man could have created such a marvel. When we deal with people, we sometimes forget how intricate the human spirit is. With observation, we find certain areas that together make up our experience of life and form a unity—a person.

One of my favorite boyhood pastimes was taking things apart. I was always happiest when I found an old clock or radio to dismantle without bringing parental wrath down on my head (not to mention other portions of my anatomy). In my tinkering, I learned that the machines I took apart consisted of many carefully made pieces that, by themselves, could do nothing. A clock, for instance, contained all kinds of little gears, wheels, and springs that fit together in a wonderful puzzle. Lying loose on my table, they amounted to little more than scrap metal. Put together by a watchmaker, they became an instrument that could turn eternity into seconds.

Likewise, we are made up of different pieces. Separated, these amount to very little. Put together by God, they form the marvelous interlocking puzzle of human life. In the third chapter of Proverbs, we find a picture of this life as it exists under the tutelage of wisdom.

The Inner Kingdom of the I

You don't have to spend much time in the Scriptures to see that there is a basic unit of personhood. For our purposes, I will call this basic unit "the inner kingdom of the I"—the unique being that exists in each person as an entity distinct from all others. Simply, it is what makes me me.

In Proverbs, we cannot help but see how pervasive and important is the interplay between this inner kingdom and the whole world of our outward experiences. What I live on the inside is affected by what happens on the outside. Even more importantly, what I experience on the outside is molded by what is going on inside. Though a strong statement, it is true. The course of my outward life *is* altered by my inner life.

Solomon couldn't have made it any clearer that the commitments of our heart make their impact on the daily course of life.

> *My son, if you accept my words and store up my commands within you . . . then you will understand the fear of the Lord and find the knowledge of God (2:1, 5 NIV).*

Storing God's commands within us creates a character that in turn earns these assurances.

> *God holds victory in store for the upright; he is a shield to those whose walk is blameless, for he guards the*

> *course of the just and protects the way of his faithful*
> *ones (2:7–8 NIV).*

Notice the interplay between our practical, day-to-day walk and the kind of character God's Word has produced in us. It is the *upright* for whom God holds victory. It is the *blameless* for whom He is a shield. He guards the course of the *just*. The *faithful* are they who receive His protection. When the inner kingdom of the I is steeped in the ways of God, the strengths of God are likewise received. What sets this whole process apart from merely human knowledge and human self-help is the direct involvement of God to create in us a character that reflects Him, where we have direct access to the very presence of God.

An even stronger affirmation for the inner kingdom's place is the establishment of a wise life—the heart of wisdom's life-code.

> *My son, do not forget my teaching, but keep my*
> *commands in your heart, for they will prolong your life*
> *many years and bring you prosperity (3:1 NIV).*

What I hold in my heart will ultimately tell the course of my life. The inner kingdom of the I is mine, given me by my Creator. It's all there really is of me, and I can choose to govern it any way I wish. But the stark fact of its existence remains: As long as I govern it on the basis of my own attempts at wisdom, I am doomed to a despot's fancy. If I look into the pool of God's Word, I will find there the true wisdom that alone will serve as a sure guide for the course of my life.

The Spheres of Outward Experience

If the roots of personhood are in the inner kingdom of the I, its branches and foliage are in life's outward experience. Every day we encounter the pell-mell rush of the milieu where we live. The soil of our soul bears fruit in the sunshine of the world about us.

Proverbs shows us three categories into which this outward experience falls: the physical circumstances of life, the relationships we maintain with others, and the relationship we maintain with God. All of us encounter life in each of these categories, and to a large degree, it is our interaction with these that sculpts the lines of our life, the portrait by which others know us.

When we say wisdom offers health and equilibrium, we are speaking in the context of these spheres. Proverbs contends that for us to be healthy, full-orbed people, each of these areas must be healthy, too. If any one of them is crippled, all of life will be marred.

Let's look at relationships with others. All of us carry with us the scars of past conflicts. It is impossible to grow up without being hurt by our parents or by our peers. As adults, we continue to be exposed to many chances for injury. If we have been consistently snubbed and treated as an outsider, we may develop a defensive posture—hating yet craving acceptance. If our trust has been betrayed, we may develop deep feelings of suspicion and cynicism. If we have learned to bend people to our own ends, we may manipulate others.

These attitudes will make their impact on all the other spheres of life. If my inner kingdom is full of anger, resentment, mistrust, and selfishness, my relationship with God will be short-circuited by my hatred of those about me. Likewise, my approach to the circumstances of life will be twisted and complicated.

Thus, our life-code, if it is to do us justice, must serve to restore and support health in each sphere of life. What has occurred in our past must be dealt with constructively and regeneratively. We need avenues of rapprochement with others and require stamina and understanding in dealing with life's circumstances. We must, above all, establish and secure an intimate relationship with God. Any life-code that fails to facilitate these vital functions is a faulty one.

These struggles are exactly what Proverbs promises. Only wisdom provides a way for each sphere to be cleansed, healed, and given an invigorating atmosphere for growth.

THE SHAPE OF WISDOM

In Proverbs 3, we can further see the lifestyle wisdom makes possible, as well as what happens when we choose another life-code. This model provides five directives concerning wisdom, followed by the results they bring if followed.

> *My son, do not forget my teaching,*
> *But let your heart keep my commandments;*
> *For length of days and years of life,*
> *And peace they will add to you.*
>
> *Do not let kindness and truth leave you;*
> *Bind them around your neck,*
> *Write them on the tablet of your heart.*
> *So you will find favor and good repute in the sight of*
>   *God and man.*
>
> *Trust in the Lord with all your heart,*
> *And do not lean on your own understanding.*
> *In all your ways acknowledge Him,*
> *And He will make your paths straight.*
>
> *Do not be wise in your own eyes;*
> *Fear the Lord and turn away from evil.*
> *It will be healing to your body,*
> *And refreshment to your bones.*
>
> *Honor the Lord from your wealth,*
> *And from the first of all your produce;*
> *So your barns will be filled with plenty,*
> *And your vats will overflow with new wine.*
>
> *My son, do not reject the discipline of the Lord,*
> *Or loathe His reproof,*
> *For whom the Lord loves He reproves,*
> *Even as a father, the son in whom he delights.*

Obedience Produces a Full Life

Speaking as God's mouthpiece to those who are willing to learn wisdom, Solomon says, "Let your heart keep my commandments" (3:1). His first concern is to establish a vital link between the inner kingdom of his hearers and the teachings of God. Until our hearts are saturated with the will and Word of God, wisdom is an empty concept.

After the command comes the promise, "If you will keep my commandments, here is what they will do for you: they will bring you length of days and years of life, and peace." The promise is not so much that God will add up totals and reward length of days and peace to those who end up with a credit on His books. Rather, entering a relationship with God produces circumstances of health, joy, and vigor. Length of days and peace are the vehicles Solomon chose to convey the blessedness of life lived in communion with God. His message was that God gives this promise, "If you will give me your heart, I will give you my joy, my peace, and my stability."

For the first directive, we have this equation: "Obedience produces a full life." Keep my commands and you will find life brimming with "pure well-being, free from all that disturbs peace and satisfaction, internal and external contentment."[1] I am always amazed at the optimism, the grandeur of the life wisdom offers. Is it really possible to have a life in which nothing destroys our peace, in which nothing mars our internal and external satisfaction? That is, indeed, the kind of life Solomon holds out in wisdom.

Kindness and Truth Produce Favor and Good Repute

The second directive is found in Proverbs 3:3–4. Having laid the foundation of a relationship between our inner kingdom and the Word of God, the teacher of wisdom says, "Do not let kindness and truth leave you; bind them around your neck, write them on the tablet of your heart."

Another version records, "Let love and faithfulness never leave you" (NIV). Kindness and truth, it seems, are not characteristics that rest naturally in our hearts. We are told, "Don't let them leave," as though they are constantly in danger of slipping away. Great pains are required to secure them to our lives. Speaking symbolically, Solomon says we must bind them around our necks where they will constantly remind us of their presence. We must write them on our hearts, so they become our natural mode of existence.

But what are kindness and truth? What was Solomon's message in this directive? It is significant that we have these two characteristics as an unseparated pair: Kindness has its meaning only in relationship to truth; truth is not whole unless it is in the presence of kindness. Although kindness and truth are not the same, they complement and complete one another.

Kindness here in the Old Testament is the equivalent of what is called agape love in the New Testament. To be kind is to adopt as our own a disposition that seeks to serve others, to improve the lot of those with whom we live. Kindness is a mother not wanting any more meat so her young, hungry son can have a second pork chop. It is a husband going out of his way to reassure and support his wife, to show her she is loved and important. Kindness is a blond, blue-eyed, eternally curious three-year-old concerned that the bug she met today on the sidewalk has someplace to sleep tonight. As a way of life, its disposition is never conveyed merely in words. Being kind spills over onto the people, the animals, and even the objects that surround us.

Kindness, though, is only one aspect of this second structure. "Do not let kindness *and truth* leave you," says the teacher. Truth, or as it is translated elsewhere as faithfulness, means firmness, trustworthiness, and stability.[2] The relationship with God breeds faithfulness, truth. Let's juxtapose the sentence. If we have no direct link with truth, we will not have the criteria to judge what is and is not kind. Kindness is a social extension of morality, and morality has its roots in truth. Truth defines kindness.

When truth finds expression in our lives, it becomes what we normally associate with faithfulness—"standing to one's promises"[3] —following through on the responsibilities we have to ourselves, to God, to our society, and specifically, to those we live with. Kindness and truth are the twin virtues that characterize a wise lifestyle and bear their fruit in the sphere of personal relationships.

After the command comes the promise. By writing kindness and truth on the tablet of your heart, "you will find favor and good repute in the sight of God and man" (3:4). Several years ago, a notion was popularized that we could, by special techniques, win friends and influence people. I have always felt a tinge of skepticism about this because I view friendship as a mutually rewarding interplay of personalities, which requires giving with no presupposed right of taking. We don't win friends; we make them. Our influence on people is solely a function of their response to our character. We will only gain the favor of other people as they see and are attracted to our character, to our disposition. What they see in us they will respond to. Kindness and truth must be the bedrock for our interrelationships. As God builds kindness and truth in us, we will find others attracted to His handiwork.

Trust Produces Cleared Paths

We have now seen two directives: obedience that produces a full life; kindness and truth that produce favor and good repute.

The third is found in Proverbs 3:5, 6. Solomon says, "Trust in the Lord with all your heart, and do not lean on your own understanding. In all your ways acknowledge him." The first directive was a foundational command. The second referred to our conduct in the sphere of relationships with people. The third deals with our relationship with God. Three principal words are used to direct that relationship. We are to *trust* Him, to *lean* on His understanding (not on our own), and to *acknowledge* Him in all ways.

It seems as though the most difficult aspect of our walk with God is to trust Him completely. Even after we have repented our sinful ways and placed our faith in Him for salvation, it is all too easy to put our trust for daily needs in those physical structures we can actually see. Yes, God supplies our needs, but the office supplies our weekly check. Yes, God is the Great Healer, but the doctors give us medicine. Yes, God's wisdom is wonderful, but for advice on how to be happily married, we can always turn to women's magazines for the latest specialist's word.

I am not suggesting an actual dichotomy exists in each of these examples. God uses our jobs to help supply our needs. He uses doctors to help heal us. He may use the advice of the latest specialist to teach us how to order our marriages. But it is all too easy to give lip service to God and put our real trust and hope in human wisdom. It has become much too easy to exchange the power of God for a cheap, impotent worldly imitation.

What happens when we lose our jobs? When our health fails? When the storms of life batter our homes? Real trust in God shines in these times. There may be tension and pain when the hardships come, but those who have learned to trust God will only find their peace and confidence growing when there is nothing left to depend on but God.

The more we trust Him, the more we are free to lean on Him. The word Solomon used in chapter three literally means "to lean with the whole body on something, in order to rest upon it and be strengthened by it."4 Trust allows us to lean on God's faithfulness.

I love to hike in the mountains. After hours of hard hiking, there is nothing so rewarding as leisurely savoring the majesty of the heights. I like to find some jutting rock and sit, just drinking in the beauty. All around is the breathtaking panorama of tumbling rock shapes, brilliant evergreens in several hues, and the air crisp and refreshing. Perched out on my ledge, I am not afraid. I have perfect trust in the rock. It will not give way beneath me. I can sit and rest for the trip back down the mountain.

Similarly, when it comes to our relationship with God, we have a choice: We can lean on our own understanding or we can lean wholly on God as He reveals His wisdom to us. Leaning on His understanding then leads us to acknowledge that every area of life must properly be in submission to Him.

After the command comes the promise. "Trust in the Lord . . . and He will make your paths straight" (3:5, 6 NIV). When Solomon said God would make our paths straight he meant that He would clear them of obstacles. John the Baptist used the same imagery with those who were to see and hear the ministry of Jesus. He told them, "Make straight the way of the Lord (John 1:23)." To paraphrase, "Get everything out of His way. Break down the walls that will hinder Him. Open up the avenues for Him to walk down. Clear away the rubble."

Thus, Solomon's message is clear: If we will trust God, we will see Him straighten out our paths. We will watch Him break down the barriers that have imprisoned us for so long. The bad habits, the limited horizons, the unbeatable temptations that cage our lives—God can clear these all away and use the rubble to build our lives afresh. His grace and His power can meet all our needs. Trust produces cleared paths.

Deference Produces Healing

Directive number four is found in verses seven and eight. Solomon picks a topic similar in language to the preceding directive. Here he says, "Do not be wise in your own eyes; fear the Lord and turn away from evil."

Remember he has just said, "Trust the Lord, lean on His understanding." Now he shifts his view from the relationship we have with God to the impact this relationship makes on our inner kingdom. More specifically, he wants to show us how we are to view ourselves in the light of our relationship with God.

How are we to relate to our own abilities? How much confidence can we place in ourselves? These are the questions the teacher addresses here. His basic answer is "Don't be wise in your own eyes." In other words, establish from the first a willingness to defer to God's wisdom. Certainly, God does not have a specific command for every little circumstance, every question we will face. Occasions will arise when we will have to exercise our own faculties of discernment. But to be wise in our own eyes is to seek instinctively our own way instead of asking, "How would God want this handled?" Wisdom teaches us to place our trust first in the counsel of God, then in our ability as it is informed by God's counsel.

After the command comes the promise. Defer to God's counsel for "it will be healing to your body, and refreshment to your bones" (3:8). Trust produces cleared paths; deference to God's wisdom produces healing. "Healing has here . . . not the meaning of restoration from sickness, but the raising up of enfeebled strength, or the confirming of that which exists."[5] Thus, deferring to God has the effect of marshaling and renewing our strength. The more we pursue our own ways, the more we fragment and drain away our strength; the more we defer to God's ways, the more we increase and channel our strength. God's grace heals us by restoring what we have destroyed by our sinful practices. God's wisdom heals us by renewing our strength in the face of every challenge. It is the Holy Spirit who enables us to trust God for the healing of grace and to experience the healing of God's wisdom.

Not only does deference give us deep reserves of spiritual strength, it also is a constant refreshment to our inner kingdom. Our resiliency, our ability to bounce back from trial and even defeat, are commodities acquired by practicing deference to God's wisdom. As long as we are depending on ourselves, every ounce of our energy will be consumed by the struggle just to survive. Instead, we must open up our lives to the resources of God's strength.

Honoring God Produces Prosperity

Finally, we come to the last directive. We have seen how wisdom affects our relations with others, with God, and with our inner kingdom. Now we will see how it affects our relationship to the circumstances of life.

Solomon's last directive is in verses nine and ten. "Honor the Lord from your wealth, and from the first of all your produce." Notice that he uses the word "honor." He doesn't say, "pay the Lord." Neither does he say specifically, "support your local temple" (although it was true that giving was done through the worship structure of the temple). He articulates a basic and central principle in the life of wisdom: Honor the Lord with all your material resources.

In the Old Testament as well as in most churches today, honoring the Lord in this way has a very specific formula. The tithe, or the tenth part of all one receives, is to be given to God through His church. Two things can be said about this practice.

First, we must realize that giving to God must indeed be an expression of honor. Our relationship with Him must find expression in the ways we use our time and material resources. To honor someone is to acknowledge his contribution to our lives.

I recently attended a school banquet where a hard-working student was honored with a gift of $500 for her dedication to the tasks set before her. In giving the gift, the school was saying, "We recognize your contribution to the school as well as your determination to make the best of your opportunities."

To honor God is to say, "I acknowledge Your impact on my life. I recognize how much I owe You. I know everything I am and have comes from Your hand." Giving to God is not trying to earn His favor so He will give us more. Rather it is being consistent in the area of our material resources with our inner commitment to spiritual truth. If God is who He claims and if He really is to us what we claim, it would be strange if this made no difference in the way we spent our material resources.

Second, notice that our honoring portion must come from our wealth, from the first of all our produce, not from that which means little to us. Giving from the leftovers mocks God. If we wish to honor someone, we give the very best we have, whatever that may be.

After the command comes the promise. "If you will honor God from your material goods, you will find your barns will be filled with plenty, and your vats will overflow with new wine" (3:10, paraphrased). Was Solomon really saying the way to get rich is to give to God? Indirectly it may happen that way, but not everyone who follows the biblical life-code will necessarily have lots of money.

Actually, Solomon says that honoring God insures our lives will prosper. His use of this imagery symbolizes plenty. To paraphrase God's promise, honor me and I will see to it that your every need is met, just as surely as if you had millions of dollars to your name in the local savings and loan. Is there any other way to obtain a more secure lifestyle? None! Anywhere!

• • ● • •

These five directives comprise the model of life governed according to wisdom. Here are wisdom's basic structures.

Model of Life Governed
According to Wisdom

The Commandment		The Promise
Obedience	produces	A Full Life
Kindness and Truth ..	produce	Favor and Good Repute
Trust	produces	Cleared Paths
Deference	produces	Healing
Honoring God	produces	Prosperity

Even though it would be hard not to see how substantial are the benefits wisdom offers, let's look at this diagram again.

If we govern our lives apart from wisdom, we will find it characterized by the very opposite of this model. If we choose *disobedience,* we will find life boiling down to emptiness. All the glittering gold Satan dangles before us will trickle away; all our dreams will become an empty siren's song.

If we allow *cruelty* and *falsehood* to reign, we will experience a life of hatred and alienation. Nothing but this is left to us apart from God. When we reject God, cruelty and falsehood are our only alternatives. Although small features of life in the beginning, they grow daily until they govern all of life.

If trust is rejected and *suspicion* of God is our normal pattern, our lives will be filled with barriers—not just obstacles—barriers. Emotional, physical, and especially spiritual barriers will be present.

If we choose *self-reliance,* we must be prepared to accept a life of weakness. When we choose to seek our own way through life, we have traded the rock for the shifting sands. Try running on loose sand— nothing else is more tiring.

And finally, when we insult Him by *hoarding* all for ourselves, we have insured for ourselves a life of destitution. Not all who reject God's wisdom will be poor in terms of dollars. Many who choose something other than wisdom are rich. But they have chosen to supply their own needs rather than allow God to provide for them. They may be rich in material wealth but destitute in the riches of peace, confidence, and security. To keep their inner destitution from eating up the rest of their lives, they grasp and hoard all the decaying wealth of this world.

Here's the model of a life governed apart from wisdom.

Model of Life Governed
Apart from Wisdom

The Choice	The Fruit
Disobedience .... produces ...	An Empty Life
Cruelty and Falsehood . produce	Hatred and Alienation
Suspicion .... produces ...	Barriers
Self-Reliance .... produces ...	Weakness
Insult .... produces ...	Destitution

Solomon begins by establishing a link between our inner kingdom and the commandments of God. In verses eleven and twelve, he speaks of an important aspect of this link, "My son, do not despise the Lord's discipline and do not resent his rebuke, because the Lord disciplines those he loves, as a father the son he delights in" (NIV).

This life I have set forth from Proverbs is not some idealistic, pie-in-the-sky dream but a practical possibility in the eyes of God. When we adopt wisdom as our life-code, we will find ourselves in the thick of life, fighting as sons of the King the enemies Satan places in this world. As this old cliché expresses it, we are no longer adrift at the mercy of life's savage forces. We have entered a relationship with the One who loves and guides us.

We see this new relationship in the reproof He gives. God disciplines those He loves—those who are His to discipline. He teaches and trains us from our first halting steps in wisdom. Discipline and reproof are God's hand at work in all our lives and our surest proof of our sonship. This is the greatest benefit of wisdom as a life-code. To adopt wisdom means to surrender ourselves to the God of the ages, to place our poor, naked quivering souls between His hands. To live by His wisdom is finally and fully to know we are loved. We have at last made a true friend and found the Father.

SOME SUGGESTIONS

Solomon has issued directions that mark the basic structures of the life lived according to wisdom. Here are some suggestions that may help you put Solomon's directions into practice.

(1) Solomon tells us that obedience to God's teaching can produce a full life. A good place to learn obedience is where you already know what you ought to do. Pick one or two of these places and practice obedience this week. Good habits are learned by practice. Obedience to the will of God can and should become a reflex of the life lived according to the biblical life-code.

(2) Solomon teaches that kindness and truth produce favor and good repute. Kindness and cruelty are habits. Find someone you see daily who is most apt to see you when you tend to be the least kind. Practice kindness to that person until you get a feel for what the habit of kindness entails. Don't excuse yourself for fatigue, business, or any other reason. There are no excuses for lack of kindness.

(3) Trust in God produces cleared paths. Probe yourself and your life. Where are your paths most obstructed? Probe deeper. Are you trusting yourself at those points? If so, acknowledge that you will have to surrender those jumbled paths to God. Every day consciously place those obstructed paths before God for Him to clear up.

(4) Deference produces healing. Most of us, no

matter how abject we may seem to others, have some hidden jewel in our psyche that we consider our greatest strength—our one redeeming asset to turn to in a crisis or for reassurance of self-worth. To defer to God, this hoarded pearl must be revealed before Him and recognized as sadly inadequate. First as an act of capitulation and then of worship, take your cherished inner asset (beauty, will power, intelligence, education, finance) and offer it to the Lord. Ask to be taught that even this is not to be loved above the counsel and the love of God.

(5) Honoring God, we are told, produces prosperity. List all of your expenditures for the past couple weeks, including charitable and church giving. Go ahead. Be honest. Then total up how much you spent for yourself (and if applicable, your family). Add up how much was spent simply to better the lot of others directly. Then total up how much was given directly to God and to His work. Now you can see how well you have honored God in your possessions. You may surprise yourself.

· • ● • ·

The biblical life-code brings us face to face with righteousness. But what exactly *is* righteousness? What does the biblical life-code teach us about friendship? How does a wise man treat money? Does Wisdom say anything about the way we use words? These are some of the questions we want to consider next.

5. Wisdom and the Image of the Righteous

Words have the power to conjure up all sorts of images, sometimes clear and delightful, sometimes fearsome. Let's try a few. What comes to mind when you hear the word "mother"? How about "Ghenghis Khan"? Not the same image I hope. How about "sizzling barbecue on a summer evening" or "an afternoon at the ball park"? Are the images flowing?

Try switching gears for a moment. What comes to mind when you hear the word "justice"? How about "holiness" or "righteousness"? Are the images clear or fuzzy?

If your images of righteousness are hazy, don't feel alone because one of the most misunderstood spiritual concepts today must be righteousness. We may, at best, assign the word to some revered figure who seems most to embody our religious ideals, whether it be Billy Graham or Mother Teresa. At worst, we may think of traits like rigidity, conservatism, and perhaps even bigotry. For many, righteousness is some fuzzy notion like holiness—a complicated set of religious ideas having little to do with today's concerns. After all, what really counts is what applies on the job, at the supermarket, at the movies, or in the science journals. Righteousness and similar words are reserved for that obscure breed of navel contemplators known variously as philosophers, theologians, and saints.

Even if we have the discernment to acknowledge that righteousness may have some place in today's world, we may be in danger of falling off into another error— thinking righteousness is primarily a set of stock responses to moral issues. For example, righteousness may come to mean being against abortion, pornography, open sex, and violence on television, or being in favor of prayer in public schools, tax credits for religious institutions, and aid for the poor. Some may even go so far as to equate righteousness with membership in a special interest group, such as the old Moral Majority or Greenpeace.

Proverbs, however, teaches an entirely different concept of righteousness. If we let Solomon instruct us, we see that righteousness concerns what we are inside, which in turn will affect what we do. We are righteous according to what we are in our inner selves.

In these next chapters, we arrive at the apex of our study. Here we explore what happens when we allow God to build in us this approach to life. We see what kind of person we can expect to become and what our lifestyle can be.

From Proverbs, I have selected several issues to give us glimpses of wisdom's lifestyle—friendship, money, conversation, which were some of the everyday concerns of life that were important to Solomon. But behind and above all of these runs one inclusive character trait that belongs exclusively to the biblical life-code. When you begin living according to wisdom, no matter what you may experience, you will begin to be a righteous person.

One of Proverbs' most helpful points is its down-to-earth portrayal of righteousness. We find Solomon's genius in his ability to give truth away in cameos, vivid little pictures that stick in the mind and heart. By compiling and superimposing these, a surprisingly clear portrait of a righteous person emerges.

The Image of the Righteous

To understand the picture presented in Proverbs, a basic distinction must be made between the wicked person and the righteous person. Solomon refers to a person by various descriptions. One person may be wise, righteous, upright, and blameless; another may be foolish, wicked, and perverse. Here are some basic definitions to help you.

The Righteous are those who have opened their hearts and minds to receive God's truth. Being open to Him, they receive His teaching and may also be called the upright, the blameless, and the wise. But they are righteous *because* they are in right relationship with God.

Wisdom is the body of truth God seeks to instill in one who is righteous or in right relation with Him.

The Wicked are those who spurn instruction, who turn away from God and thus do not learn wisdom. Consequently, they may be called foolish, crooked, evil, and perverse. These persons are wicked *because* they are turned from God and being so, they cannot learn wisdom.

· • ● • ·

Remembering these, let's study more closely the portrait of the righteous person. Solomon offers us the profile not only of righteousness but also of wickedness. The following presents the character traits involved and a life situation where these traits may be called to operate.

Are you ready?

The righteous man is upright (2:7, 21; 3:32; 11:5, 11, 20; 14:2, 8–9; 20:11; 21:8; 30:12).

We see that his conduct is said to be pure. Some synonyms of upright are conscientious, scrupulous, and honorable. One who is upright acts with integrity because his conduct is governed by an inner commitment to rightness.

The wicked man is perverse (2:13–14; 6:12–14; 8:8; 10:32; 11:20; 14:2; 15:26, 28; 19:16; 28:14).

We read that his loves tend toward evil, toward darkness rather than light. He is steadfastly turned away from God and God's ways, providing a contrast to the upright man's course.

Fifty-five-year-old Arnold suffers from chronically poor health. Five years ago, his doctor offered to perform a surgery that held small chance of helping (certainly no guarantee of curing) Arnold's malady. He clearly presented it only as an option he was willing to try if Arnold wished. Desperate, Arnold gave the requisite approval, and surgery was performed.

In the five subsequent years, the problem has not disappeared. The surgery did nothing, except cost Arnold discomfort and money. In his personal contacts, Arnold has been approached discreetly by a lawyer who urges him to file a malpractice suit against the doctor for unnecessary and irresponsible surgery. The lawyer assures Arnold he has an airtight case and would stand to gain much money from the doctor's malpractice insurance.

What would an upright man do? A perverse man?

· · ● · ·

The righteous man is kind (10:12; 11:17, 23; 12:10; 14:14, 22; 16:6; 21:26).

The righteous life is marked by generosity. These people are merciful, return good when they are wronged, try to suspend judgment whenever possible, and forego revenge. They love, that is, they seek the good of others.

The wicked are violent (2:22; 3:31; 6:12–14; 11:9, 11, 17; 12:6, 10, 26).

The wicked are progenitors of strife. They are treacherous and cruel, tearing down rather than building up.

Karen works hard at her executive position in an advertising firm. By an unfortunate slip, she all but destroyed one high-paying account. With hard work and at great personal pain, she labored to put the situation right. After many weeks, she now feels she's on the verge of repairing the situation.

Ron observed Karen's gaff with interest. He knew that if it were to come to the attention of their superior, it would seriously hamper Karen's chances of advancement. Since they were members of the same department, he knew they would inevitably butt heads for the next promotion. Ron felt Karen's sex gave her an unfair advantage. Perhaps he should even the decks a bit.

How would a righteous person react in this situation?

· • ● • ·

The righteous man is truthful (8:7–8; 10:9; 11:3; 12:19; 13:5, 17; 14:5, 22, 25).

He is of unquestionable integrity and thus makes a good witness. He is worthy of the trust he incites in his associates.

The righteous man is just (2:7–8; 8:20; 11:1; 12:5; 20:10; 21:15; 29:7).

He sees and defends the rights of the poor and disenfranchised. In all his dealings, he acts in good faith.

The wicked are false (2:15; 3:32; 6:12–14; 8:8; 14:2; 28:13, 18).

He is crooked and devious. He may put on a good front, but behind it, he is cunning and devoid of integrity.

Anthony's sales position kept him on the road an average of four days of the week. Sometimes he would even be gone two and three weeks at a stretch. His absence posed two problems, one for him and one for his wife, Nancy. His dilemma was the complete freedom his company gave him with his expense account. The opportunity presented itself regularly to turn in bogus expenses as a means of gaining that bit of extra income needed for the expenses at home. Nancy's problem was her loneliness and frustration in handling the home by herself, which was heightened by her neighbor. Being single, he always came over at the right moments ready to help and could turn a phrase with unfair skill.

How would a righteous man conduct himself in these situations? A righteous woman?

• • ● • •

The righteous man is meditative (12:8; 15:28).

He gives serious consideration to the course of his life. As a result, he is blessed not just with sight, but with insight. He does not simply watch the events of life rush past him but searches for meaning in them and plucks out of each one something to strengthen and deepen him.

The righteous man is hopeful (10:28; 29:6).

He is not habitually downcast but looks forward with anticipation and joy because his hope is eternal.

The wicked are arrogant (8:13; 10:2–3; 11:28; 15:25; 16:5).

Far from seeking insight and direction as he faces life, he is convinced of his own sufficiency. He is greedy and trusts only in his own wealth. Because these are not enough, he falls easily to cynicism and despair when what he has trusted fails.

Jason shoved open the door of the fraternity-house lounge and flopped on the couch. The week's classes had filled his head with whirling, confusing ideas. His sociology professor had talked at length of the pressures of the world's overpopulation. His economics professor spoke of the imminent danger of the world economy's collapse. In biology class, they had read the awesome possibilities of genetic research.

To unwind, he snapped on the TV. The newscaster reported war, economic problems, political issues, crime statistics, and the increasing world hunger plight. With a sigh, he heaved himself from the couch and ambled over to the pop machine. *Something cold to drink might help— maybe stronger than pop,* he thought.

How would righteousness help Jason? What are his options if he rejects righteousness or is ignorant of it?

· • ● • ·

On Becoming Righteous

We have seen the image of righteousness Solomon would like us to acquire. Life is better for the righteous, he tells us. Uprightness, kindness, truthfulness, justice, meditation, and hope are not static, musty ideas, which are impotent in the face of today's complexity. They are the way life ought to be lived.

As is always the case, Solomon does not simply tell us what we might become—righteous—but he also outlines what we must do. To summarize Proverbs, look at this kernel of truth, found at the root of all Solomon teaches.

> *To become righteous requires a transformation of our inner lives so we are oriented toward the teaching of God instead of toward our own choices.*

Remembering this, let's explore in more detail how Jason, Anthony, Nancy, Karen, Ron, and Arnold can benefit by learning righteousness.

In Proverbs, when someone is called righteous, a statement is being made about his orientation toward the teaching of God. The righteous person is open, concerned, diligent, and faithful to what he receives. His life reflects more and more the characteristics associated with wisdom. Therefore, the righteous person has opened his heart and life to God's truth. Wisdom is that body of truth that God desires to instill in those who will learn.

Let's peruse these verses that lend insight.

> *Hear, my son, and accept my sayings,*
> *And the years of your life will be many.*
>
> *I have directed you in the way of wisdom;*
> *I have led you in upright paths.*
>
> *When you walk, your steps will not be impeded;*
> *And if you run, you will not stumble.*
>
> *Take hold of instruction; do not let go.*
> *Guard her, for she is your life.*
>
> *Do not enter the path of the wicked,*
> *And do not proceed in the way of evil men (4:10–14).*
>
> *For they eat the bread of wickedness,*
> *And drink the wine of violence.*
>
> *But the path of the righteous is like the light of dawn,*
> *That shines brighter and brighter until the full day*
> *(4:17–18).*

If we want to learn wisdom, we must "take hold of instruction" as it comes through God's Word. The two ways we may take are clearly delineated in this passage:

the way of the wicked, which precludes learning wisdom, and the way of the righteous, which gains more and more the illumination of wisdom and of God's presence.

In Solomon's words, "The fear of the Lord is the beginning of wisdom, and the knowledge of the Holy One is understanding" (9:10). As we fear God, as He has access to our lives, He can pour into us His wisdom. As we come to know the Holy One, all the vistas of true understanding spread themselves before us.

Here's a marvelous dialogue from George MacDonald's *The Fisherman's Lady* that illustrates what must happen in us to make us righteous.

This dialogue is between the marquis, one of the book's main characters, and Mr. Graham, a schoolteacher with keen spiritual sight, in nineteenth-century Scotland.

"Sit down, sir," said the marquis courteously, pleased with the calm and unobtrusive bearing of the man. "They tell me I'm dying, Mr. Graham."

"I'm sorry it seems to trouble you, my lord."

"What! Wouldn't it trouble you, then?"

"I don't think so, my lord."

"Ah! You're one of the elect, no doubt?"

"That's a thing I never did think about, my lord."

"What do you think about, then?"

"About God."

"And when you die you'll go straight to heaven, of course."

"I don't know, my lord. That's another thing I never trouble my head about."

"Ah, you're like me then. I don't care much about going to heaven. What do you care about?"

"The will of God. I hope your lordship will say the same."

"No, I won't. I want my own will."

"Well, that is to be had, my lord."

"How?"

"By taking His will for yours as the better of the two, which it must be in every way."

"That's all moonshine!"

"It is light, my lord."

"Well, I don't mind confessing, if I am to die, I should prefer heaven to the other place, but I trust I have no chance of either. Do you now honestly believe there are two such places?"

"I don't know, my lord."

"You don't know! And you come here to comfort a dying man?"

"Your lordship must first tell me what you mean by 'two such places.' And as to comfort, going by my notions, I cannot tell which you would be more or less comfortable in; and that, I presume, would be the main point with your lordship."

"And what, pray sir, would be the main point with you?"

"To get nearer to God."

"Well, I can't say I want to get nearer to God. It's little He's ever done for me."

"It's a good deal He has tried to do for you, my lord."

"Who's interfered? What stood in His way, then?"

"Yourself, my lord."[1]

In these few sparkling lines, we see the predicament we all face. We do not like where our own choices—our self-made life-codes—bring us, but neither do we wish to accept the will of God. We, only we, stand in the way of our own happiness.

MacDonald further shows us the solution to this problem.

It was Mr. Graham who broke the silence that followed.

"Are you satisfied with yourself, my lord?"

"No, by George!"

"You would like to be better?"

"I would."

"Then you are of the same mind with God."

"Yes, but I'm not a fool. It won't do to say I should like to be, I must be, and that's not so easy. It's too hard to be good. I would have to fight for it, but there's no time. How is a poor devil to get out of such an infernal scrape?"

"Keep the Commandments."

"That's it, of course. But there's not time, I tell you—no time! At least that's what those cursed doctors will keep telling me."

"If there were but time to draw another breath, there would be time to begin."

"How am I to begin? Which am I to begin with?"

"There is one commandment that includes all the rest."

"Which is that?"

"To believe in the Lord Jesus Christ."

"That's cant!"

"After thirty years' trial of it, it is to me the essence of wisdom. It has given me a peace which makes life or death all but indifferent to me."

"What am I to believe about Him, then?"

"You are to believe *in* Him, not *about* Him."

"I don't understand."

"He is our Lord and Master, Elder Brother, King, Saviour, the Divine Man, the human God. To believe in Him is to give ourselves up to Him in obedience—to search out His will and do it."[2]

· • ● • ·

If we were to stop here, we would know how to begin on the way of righteousness, but we would miss a wealth of insight into the life of righteousness Solomon has to share. Now let's see what happens once we take on this life.

The Righteous and Their Peers

An intriguing aura surrounds the righteous in their relationship with the people around them. Most of us enjoy being well-liked and respected by our peers. Something in us responds when people seek us out at parties and when our opinions are heard and repeated. According to Solomon, the qualities God builds into the character of the righteous make them attractive to their peers. They may not be flashy or bubbly, certainly not overbearing, but something exists in these folks that draws others to them.

Solomon shows that at least part of this magnetism lies in the blessing righteous people inevitably shower on those around them. The wicked person destroys others by his pride and falsehood. In seeking always to push himself forward, he smothers them. The righteous man never seeks to be destructive of his peers but wants to build others up, to bring hope and joy where there is none. He tries to draw the best out of his associates, not criticize harshly and act out of habitual suspicion.

Nothing serves as a better indicator of our true spiritual condition than the effect we have on our peers. No matter how lofty our ideals or how great our claims, if we are a source of ruin to those about us, we are not righteous. People see God and feel His love when a righteous person is among them.

Here's what Proverbs says about the impact a righteous man has on his peers.

> *Righteous lips are the delight of kings, and he who speaks right is loved (16:13).*

> *The blessings God pours on the upright benefit the whole community in which they live (11:11,* paraphrased). What God accomplishes through them is to the good of all.

> *When the righteous increase, people are happier (29:2,* paraphrased). Who wouldn't be happier living in a town filled with people who were upright, kind, truthful, just, thoughtful, and hopeful?

Righteousness exalts a nation (14:34). If a nation stumbles, the trouble may well lie in its having forsaken the strength of God's ways.

One may depend upon and find comfort in the light shining in the lives of the righteous (13:9, paraphrased). The wicked? Just when you need it most, their "light" goes out.

The mouth of the righteous is a fountain of life (10:11). Everyone around is blessed by its stream.

The lips of the righteous feed many (10:21). They are a source of insight, understanding, and strength.

How about a quick self-test? Answer the questions below to evaluate your progress in the life of righteousness.

(1) The response I try to convey when I hear the opinions of others is one of
     a. respect and attentiveness.
     b. critical evaluation.
     c. scorn.

(2) If my associates were to acquire more of my characteristics today, they would
     a. be more tense and anxious.
     b. be more open and caring of others.
     c. be more at ease and optimistic.
     d. be more suspicious and closed to others.

(3) I find that those who rub shoulders with me often
     a. seem to show confidence in me by asking my opinions and help when possible.
     b. seem to tolerate my presence.
     c. seem to mistrust me.

(4) In the past year, I have given comfort and encouragement to my associates
     a. a few times.
     b. never.

c. rather often.

(5) The effect of my presence at my home/business/school is
a. to spread joy and confidence in life.
b. to cultivate honesty and fairness.
c. to encourage unhappiness and cynicism.

So, what do you think? Is your impact on others more like that of the righteous or of the wicked? This is an area even the most seasoned saint would do well to contemplate and update often.

The Confidence of the Righteous

Perhaps much of the blessing the lives of the righteous shower on their peers comes from the strength they find in God. In Proverbs, there is not the slightest hint of a despairing, defeated, uncertain child of God. Everything is strength, boldness, confidence, and peace of mind. Although there is always room for the occasional bad day in the life of the one filled with wisdom, it is never nor should ever be the norm. When God fills our lives, no room is left for despair. Only when we allow other things to take His place, do we begin to quail before the challenges of life. According to Solomon, *even their failures* are no cause for despair to the righteous.

Listen to Solomon:

The righteous will never be shaken (10:30).

The root of the righteous will not be moved (12:3).

The house of the righteous will stand (12:7).

The upright will live in the land, and the blameless will remain in it (2:21).

A righteous man falls seven times and rises again (24:16). Even his failures are not occasions of defeat. He keeps on going.

The wicked flee when no one is pursuing, but the righteous are bold as a lion (28:1).

73

> *The righteous will escape from trouble (12:13).*
>
> *The Lord will be your confidence, and will keep your foot from being caught (3:26).*
>
> *In the fear of the Lord there is strong confidence, and His children will have refuge (14:26).*
>
> *He is a shield to those who walk in integrity (2:7).*
>
> *When a man's ways are pleasing to the Lord, He makes even his enemies to be at peace with him (16:7).*
>
> *The Lord will not allow the righteous to hunger (10:3).*
>
> *The fear of the Lord leads to life, so that one may sleep satisfied, untouched [not visited] by evil (19:23).*

For those who have opened their lives to God, there is no lack of confidence. Our problems come when we try to find strength only in ourselves. We are flawed. By our own conscience, we condemn ourselves. We know by our failures, our hurts, and our times of despair that we can never create true confidence. The tragedy comes when we assume life holds no sure source of strength. It does. God is our confidence. His strength becomes ours not just in theory but in practice, day by day.

What are the dominant themes of your daily life? Contentment? Fear? Courage? Solomon leaves us no doubt that even though we may have fears and perplexities when we are righteous, we are not defeated because we have supreme confidence in God.

The Riches of the Righteous

Rewards in the life of the righteous are promised to us. We should feel comfortable receiving them from God. If He were to hand me a blank sheet of paper with orders to draw up a list of all I would like Him to do for me, I think I should feel presumptuous listing what the Proverbs promise. Look!

> *God blesses the dwelling of the righteous (3:33).*
>
> *He who sows righteousness gets a true reward (11:18).*

The righteous will be rewarded in the earth (11:21, paraphrased).

He who gives attention to the word shall find good (16:20).

Blessed is he who trusts in the Lord (16:20).

No harm befalls the righteous (12:21).

He who is steadfast in righteousness will attain to life (11:19).

The wages of the righteous is life (10:16).

The fruit of the righteous is a tree of life (11:30).

He who pursues righteousness and loyalty finds life, righteousness, and honor (21:21).

The desire of the righteous will be granted (10:24).

The tent of the upright will flourish (14:11).

The Lord will not allow the righteous to hunger (10:3).

The righteous will be rewarded with prosperity (13:21).

The righteous has enough to satisfy his appetite (13:25).

Much wealth is in the house of the righteous (15:6).

The blessings promised are inclusive and sure. They seem better than life itself. As I read them, the specters of hunger and poverty raise themselves, and I cannot help but ask myself, *What about those who do suffer from harm, poverty, or hunger? Is Solomon saying God's will is for every righteous person to be rich?*

As righteous people, God controls and is the central joy of our lives. We do not look to the things of this world to find our deepest joy. Thus, we can sincerely say with the apostle Paul, "I have learned to be content in whatever circumstances I am. I know how to get along with humble means, and I know how to live in prosperity; in any and every circumstance I have learned the secret of being filled and going hungry, both of having abundance and suffering need. I can do all things through Him who strengthens me." (Phil. 4:11–13)

Not all the righteous will be materially wealthy nor will they all escape the tragedies that are a part of life. Still the truth Solomon recognizes remains intact. God is trustworthy and blesses those who trust Him. Solomon's point is thus: All of God's children, even the poor and hungry, can call on His riches. God's treasury knows no lack. Almost all of us suffer at some time. But precisely in those times of suffering, we can look with confidence to God to meet our needs, since we know He will meet our needs.

These promises help us recall a familiar chorus.

He owns the cattle on a thousand hills,
The wealth in every mine.
He owns the rivers and the rocks and rills,
The sun and stars that shine.
Wonderful riches, more than tongue can tell,
He's my Father, so they're mine as well.
He owns the cattle on a thousand hills
I know that He will care for me.[3]

God Walks with the Righteous

A final blessing is promised to the righteous. Solomon tells us the righteous are a source of encouragement to those about them. They have the strength of God as their confidence and the wealth of God at their disposal. But most precious of all, they have the assurance that God Himself will walk beside them day by day to light the path with His presence. Other joys, other dividends pale to insignificance in the light of this blessing.

He loves him who pursues righteousness (15:9).

He hears the prayer of the righteous (15:29).

He is intimate with the upright (3:32). His private counsel is theirs.

The path of the righteous is like the light of dawn, that shines brighter and brighter until the full day (4:18).

I can think of no other blessing I would rather have. If all the others were taken and only this left, it would be enough. To have God to light the murky hours of my doubting, to put His arm around me when I'm lonely, in my black nights of grief to show me the morning breaking, to point out stepping stones through my swamps, to walk my sandy beaches, to run nimbly with me on the bracing mountain heights, and then to stand smiling on the farther shore as I make my final pilgrimage—that is enough for me. How awesome, yet how comforting are these simple words, "God walks with us."

MASTERING THE DISCIPLINES OF RIGHTEOUSNESS

Righteousness may be ours, but for it to be so, the disciplines it entails must be mastered. These will require some concrete, specific work to make the wisdom righteousness affords us the norm for our lives. Here are some ideas and some practical exercises to help you gain the disciplines of righteousness.

(1) First, recognize that righteousness is nothing more or less than the presence of God in your life. Study those whom the Bible presents as righteous (Abraham, Moses, David, Mary, Stephen, Paul, Peter) and notice how the central aspect of their spiritual life was a living relationship with God. This is what we need to become righteous.

(2) Spend time cultivating spiritual perception. Spiritual acuity is a habit, so it is acquired with regular use. Turn off some of the pipelines that dump worldly influence and perspectives into your life (i.e., for a time see what happens when you cut down on consumption of TV, movies, newspapers, secular magazines). Regulate more closely what your mind and heart consume each day. Then open new channels for the Holy Spirit to deliver enhanced spiritual awareness. Read your Bible more and more frequently. Spend time in meditation as often as possible. Expose yourself to the classics of Christian devotional literature, placing the most emphasis on volumes that help you see and interact with God. Pray frequently, spe-

cifically, and sincerely about the spiritual condition of your life. Shortly, you will find new awareness of spiritual things growing in you.

(3) Next, devote several days to a study of each of the attributes as they are described here (uprightness, kindness, truthfulness, justice, thoughtfulness, and hopefulness). Buy or borrow a topical Bible (e.g., *The New Compact Topical Bible* by Zondervan) to study references cited for these spiritual attributes. Your aim is twofold: (a) to understand clearly what each attribute entails for *practice* in daily life, and (b) to gain sensitivity to the presence or lack of these attributes in your life.

(4) During each day of study, spend time asking yourself how you have done that day with the attribute you have been studying. Have you put it into practice? Have you seen glaring instances of failure? When you see these, present them specifically as such to the Lord. Repent of them, ask His pardon, and ask for grace not to repeat the failure. Keep this process up until it becomes a natural part of your walk with God. The most mature saint may still grow in kindness, or in thoughtfulness, or in hopefulness, or in a multitude of ways secondary to these attributes.

Time spent this way is time well spent. Most comforting of all is the assurance we have that we are actually entering into daily conversation with the eternal God who made us. His promise remains: To our efforts He adds His grace and to our feeble attempts to follow the path of righteousness He adds His strength until by His help we do truly grow into the earthly image of His righteousness. Twentieth-century saints are God's only method to make righteousness relevant today.

6. Wisdom and Friendship

Two lively, lovely little girls add spice and variety to our home. With them, life is anything but boring. My wife and I are sometimes overwhelmed by the amount of joy (and occasionally the amount of anxiety!) these two little souls can produce. They are an endless source of amusement, fatigue, inspiration, and love. Now and then, out of the blue, they teach us lessons we thought we had learned long ago.

One day, we were relaxing together at home with nothing much to do. It didn't take long for our youngest to install herself on her mommy's lap, where she basked in all the direct attention she could get. Being close by, I joined in the fun, and before long, the three of us were laughing and enjoying each other's company enormously. About that time, our oldest daughter rounded the corner from her room, stopped, and took in the scene. Her big blue eyes got serious, then her lower lip jutted out. In a voice full of genuine concern, she said, "But I don't have anyone to be my friend."

In her childish way, she hit the cry of our times right on the head. Life is nothing without those whom we love and those who love us. The need for friendship is an expression of the image of God in man—something fundamental in our nature and an essential part of our being. If we lose touch with those about us, we lose something vital. God not only made man for fellowship with Himself but also for fellowship with his neighbors. Alienated from God, we lose the moorings of our lives; alienated from each other, we are deeply injured.

That's what has happened to us! Sin has placed a gulf between us and God, ripping so deeply into the fabric of human relationships that we teeter perpetually on a precarious balance between hate and love, selfishness and kindness, war and peace. Because we need human relationships so much, we search hungrily for shreds of acceptance and cling to them, sometimes at great cost. Although we wander the crammed mazes of our cities, brushing shoulders with people who have our same fear of isolation, we find it all but impossible to reach out and befriend them. Even in our churches, we hold out tidbits of our lives and wait with darting eyes for that one word of understanding and love that will rescue us from our island exile. Sadly, it so seldom comes that we outwardly play the current games and laugh on cue, but deep within, our child's voice keeps crying, "But I don't have anyone to be my friend."

Have I painted too dark a picture? I don't think so. Not long ago, I picked up a well-known national magazine and was deeply moved by an eloquent article about the growing epidemic of loneliness. People are desperately lonely: Many have failed at marriage, find little security in their professions, and their families are not a source of strength. Since ours is such a mobile culture, any sense of community tends to be obliterated. Where do they turn?

There are no simple answers. Anyone who has had his life shattered by an angry divorce will always bear the scars. Alienation is not reversed in the ten easy steps we have come to expect. But there are answers. The Bible sees man's alienation from his neighbors as a function of his sinfulness. Since we have an answer for sin, we have an answer for alienation. Looking at the life of wisdom, we find how we can be reconciled with each other. Healthy relationships are a by-product of wisdom because wisdom is built essentially on a restored relationship with God. To know God is to know what love is. To live for Him is to live His love. Therefore, living in harmony with God enables us to live in harmony with those around us.

In this chapter, we will delve into the treasury of insight Proverbs gives for lasting, fulfilling relationships.

FRIENDS WE NEED

Why do we so need interaction with others? What do our relationships give us that we wouldn't otherwise have?

Those questions will be answered implicitly in a number of ways in this chapter. Proverbs gives at least four explicit reasons for the importance of healthy relationships. Perhaps most importantly, we must understand we do not live according to wisdom outside the context of our neighborhood because it is impossible to serve God outside the social context. We must never assume that serving God is a matter of private religion. Far from it! Serving God involves us inextricably with people and since wisdom is an outgrowth of a relationship with God, it makes a tremendous impact on all our relationships. When we choose to follow the life-code Proverbs recommends, we commit ourselves to building and maintaining viable contacts with others.

Your neighborhood—those people with whom you live and work—is exactly the place where your commitment to God's way of life must be proven.

· • ● • ·

A false balance is an abomination to the Lord, but a just weight is His delight (11:1).

A just balance and scales belong to the Lord, all the weights of the bag are His concern (16:11).

At first glance, we may not catch the significance of these verses, but closer inspection reveals the connection. Solomon buys his corn meal at the corner grocery for the week. If the grocer has his scales rigged to cheat the customer, he not only wrongs the man but sins against God. The weights of the bag used to measure out produce are of concern to God because He is interested in the way we treat each other. Dishonesty is a sin because it breaks God's moral law and injures people.

When we decide to live God's way, we are in reality deciding at that very moment to treat our neighbors a certain way. To keep our walk with God in one section of our life and treat our neighbors any way we please is nonsense. We have no walk with God other than the one seen in our actions every day among our neighbors.

Two passages in the New Testament underscore this connection between our walk with God and our life with our neighbors. Jesus was asked, "Which is the great commandment in the Law?" In other words, if you were to pick from all the religious teaching of the Old Testament the one greatest commandment, what would it be? Jesus' answer was twofold. "You shall love the Lord your God with all your heart, and with all your soul, and with all your mind. This is the great and foremost commandment. And a second is like it, you shall love your neighbor as yourself" (Matt. 22:37–39). No question about it! You cannot separate love for God from love for your neighbors.

Another example is from James. "This is pure and undefiled religion in the sight of our God and Father, to visit orphans and widows in their distress, and to keep oneself unstained by the world" (James 1:27). What is pure religion? It is personal holiness (positive responses to God's commands) and compassionate care of the needy around us.

Relationships are important because they are the field in which our walk with God is practiced. The next time you are tempted to snub someone who is slow and a bit out of it, remember that that snub will be the expression of your walk with God. If you are tempted to take advantage of another's ignorance or weakness, remember that your action will be an accurate reflection of what your heart is like. Words alone do not reveal our spiritual maturity. Our claims have a quarter of the value of our deeds.

A second reason is given in Proverbs for the importance of interpersonal relationships: In them we have a tool to sharpen and strengthen one another. We have a marvelous image in chapter twenty-seven that shows what takes place in the interchange of personalities.

> *Iron sharpens iron,*
> *So one man sharpens another (27:17).*

Our walk with God is meaningless apart from the social context. Similarly, our completeness as people cannot be accomplished outside that context. "A recluse is always a very one-sided man![1] To become mature, we need the give and take of life. Though we may chafe at the irritations of living with people, it is by those very irritations that we grow. Our intercourse with each other forms our habits and our character, cultivating and polishing our manner of life, rubbing off our ruggedness and rounding our corners.[2] Just as iron can be used to shape iron, so one person may be of invaluable service to another in shaping and strengthening his life.

A friend once told me how this happened to him. He is an Englishman who had migrated to Canada in search of a better job. After arriving in his new country, he established himself as a hard-working employee and began making his way up the corporate ladder. Not finding the kind of fulfillment he had sought, he ventured out in a business of his own. His risk proved successful, and soon he was putting multiplied hours into his life's dream.

One of his employees happened to be a believer. Day after day, she read her Bible on lunch break and left other silent witnesses to her faith in Christ. The witness of this employee finally caught my friend's heart. In time, he gave his own life to the Lord. A great change had been caused through the silent, daily interaction with a believer.

He was to experience even more growth through interaction with others. As he settled into a church, he began to learn more of what it meant to live the Christian life. It happened that he was forced to work with a German man and found it extremely difficult to maintain a loving attitude toward him. Having lived through World War II and seen the destruction of so much that he loved, he had come to hold a strong prejudice against all Germans. Besides, the man was personally offensive. But knowing he had to keep loving him in the Lord, my friend kept working to maintain a good relationship. He concluded his story by telling me that this struggle to understand and accept someone he did not like was one of the best learning experiences he had ever had. He matured as he put God's truth into practice.

Interaction, then, is a tool for learning the life of wisdom. Yes, it can be hard to accept a spouse's insensitivity without resentment. Neither is it easy to work with people whose personalities run so counter to our own. But these are the chances we have to practice true love, the opportunities to learn about the power of God's redemptive grace as it works in our lives and our neighbors'.

Of course, not all learning is unpleasant. At the other end of the spectrum are those wonderfully stimulating friendships without which we would be so much poorer. For these, we must always be grateful.

Proverbs 12 gives us a third reason for the importance of relationships: Our friends may mediate our conflicts and be valuable sources of encouragement and guidance.

*Deceit is in the heart of those who devise evil, but
counselors of peace have joy (12:20).*

A counselor of peace does all he can to produce
harmony and well-being. He does not just sit on the
sidelines offering armchair advice but gets involved with
the lives of his friends, helping them through their struggles. His aim is to produce a lasting and true joy.

Many times we need just such a friend to help us
through a difficult time. Being too close to the knotty
problems that strew themselves across our paths, we often
cannot see the solutions. If we have someone we can trust
without reservation to help us along the path to peace, we
have a valuable asset.

As a pastor, one of my most rewarding ministries
was with people who would take me into their lives, show
me their struggles, and give me the chance to pray with
them for solutions. I had the joy of helping those who were
struggling with their marriages. Some allowed me to help
them take new steps in their walk with God.

On the whole, relationships are important because
we are social creatures. God has so made us that we need
each other. One of Satan's main targets is this very area.
He loves to divide friends, to destroy fellowship because
he knows how much we need each other. Even when we
do not realize this dependency, it is still there. Proverbs
tells us about it often.

*Without consultation, plans are frustrated, but with
many counselors they succeed (15:22).*

*Oil and perfume make the heart glad, so a man's
counsel is sweet to his friend (27:9).*

The interaction of daily life is an integral part of our
spiritual and emotional equilibrium. This give and take is
the arena where our walk with God is practiced, the
potter's wheel where we are molded. By convincing us we
can succeed in our own way of life, the devil is all too often
able to frustrate our friendships. However, as a source of

valuable encouragement and guidance, healthy relationships are one of wisdom's most treasured by-products.

Our Associations Mold Our Personalities

Since it is such a practical book, Proverbs is a gold mine of advice about how our relationships ought to be conducted. Living according to wisdom, we receive new freedom in personal relationships. We get new tools with which to build and maintain them.

Many of us will remember the anguished look in our parents' eyes when we bolted going out the door on the way to the latest party. Parents seem to have an inordinate desire to know where, when, why, how, but most of all who! "Who are you going to be with? Who will bring you home? Who will your friends be?" they ask. And kids seldom see the reason for the questions and often are resentful. "You mean I've got to bring all my friends home so you and Dad can pass judgment on them? What is this, the army?"

Parents, though often woefully out of touch (thankfully!) with the latest fads, have an uncanny grasp of the enduring practical realities of life: Our friends mold our personalities. Dad wants to know who his child is out with because he knows the group will have a profound impact on his child's behavior. This principle remains true even when those delightful, painful days of adolescence have turned into hazy memories. Our friends and associates both reflect and shape our thoughts, our speech, our values, and our appearance. They can be live, face-to-face associations or secondhand associations made through the movies, television, and the printed page. The strength of television as a social manipulator can be traced at least in part to this principle.

Here is what Proverbs has to say.

> *My son, if sinners entice you, do not consent. . . . My son, do not walk in the way with them (1:10, 15).*

> *He who walks with wise men will be wise, but the companion of fools will suffer harm (13:20).*
>
> *Leave the presence of a fool, or you will not discern words of knowledge (14:7).*
>
> *Do not associate with a man given to anger; or go with a hot-tempered man, lest you learn his ways, and find a snare for yourself (22:24–25).*

We tend to become like those with whom we spend time. Thus, one of the more important decisions we face is the choice of folks with whom we pursue friendship. As a normal course of life, we must associate with all kinds of people. There is, though, that one special group to which we crave admission. If the character of the people in this group runs counter to what wisdom teaches, we should choose another. We only create tension for ourselves by forming our strongest alliances with people who do not share our values.

For this reason as well, we should place some regulation on our secondhand associations. We must never assume that the friends we know only by means of the tube, the silver screen, or the pages of a book have no impact on our lives. They do! Under the best of conditions, we are extremely susceptible to role models. When these have the added impetus of wealth, glamour, power, and fun, we follow them all the more readily. I am not saying when we commit to wisdom's way, we automatically stop reading books, watching television, or going to the movies. Such decisions each of us makes individually as God teaches us. I am saying whatever we do, our associations must be subject to a regulating hand. We should always evaluate the life-code presented to see how it differs from ours.

The New Testament gives us further instruction here. Jesus spent His time with sinners, those considered the worst of the lot in that day. He did not shun the supposedly righteous for He taught in the synagogues and in the temple. Many a scribe, Pharisee, and Sadducee knew Jesus personally. Yet Jesus seemed to seek out the refugees of society—the poor, the lepers, the prostitutes, the tax collectors. In each of these associations, He was a redemptive presence. Where did He go for friendship? To Peter, John, and James—His closest circle.

We will find no better model for our associations. We contact all sorts of people in the course of our lives. Some are nice; some aren't. Some share our values; some don't. In all relationships, ours should be a redemptive presence. That person you dislike may never be the same if she could see in your life a humble but vibrant example of God's love reaching out to her. Our friendships not only mold and reflect us, but they also mold and reflect on others.

FRIENDSHIP'S HIDDEN MOTIVATORS

We will benefit by grasping another general observation from Proverbs. Friendships are not hatched in laboratories and carried to maturity in "clean rooms." They are born and grow in the milieu of everyday life. We each come to a friendship with our own needs. All of our particular desires, weaknesses, and strengths play their part in making each friendship what it is. Each friendship will always be an expression of the personalities involved.

Although expressed in Proverbs somewhat indirectly, Solomon recognizes a universal phenomenon with something like wry humor. At the same time, a sort of sadness tinges these proverbs.

> *The poor is hated even by his neighbor, but those who love the rich are many (14:20).*

> *Many will entreat the favor of a generous man, and every man is a friend to him who gives gifts (19:6).*

> *All the brothers of a poor man hate him; how much more do his friends go far from him! He pursues them with words, but they are gone (19:7).*

On the surface, we really don't learn much from these proverbs that we didn't already know. For some reason, wealth attracts friendship but not true friendship. The relationships it attracts are born of a mercenary motivation and last only as long as something is to be gained by them. Pity the one who can offer nothing but himself. He pursues his brothers with words and offers them the keys to his soul when they really want the jingle of coins. Even though he pursues them, they are gone. So wealth draws fickle attention to itself.

Let's look closer for an underlying lesson here. I think we can never divorce true friendship from the soul of those who seek it. We come to all friendships with some underlying need and seek to find the answer for that need in the friendship. If we don't recognize the presence of these underlying motivators and learn to control them, they will dictate the dimensions of all our friendships.

Many people have a bottomless need for genuine acceptance and approval. Often friendship is formed with the secret hope that here will be one person who will see our hidden worth and accept us as we are. This hidden motivator can move our friendship in one of two ways: It may make us monopolistic of our friend's time and interest, manipulative of his love, or it may turn us into spineless, simpering persons, unwilling to risk rejection by asserting even the most innocent expression of our unique character. True friendship will not last long in either of these cases. But if we can recognize and come to grips with this underlying motivator, we can use it wisely. We may see that each of our friends has his own area of need and be better equipped to meet those needs. Further, we may be better able to regulate the expectations and demands we will make in the friendship.

True friendship is something we normally reserve for a select few because it involves the keys to our most private reserves. Our best relationships are neither built on some mercenary expectation nor are they unaware of the primary needs we all bring to friendship. Our closest friends are those who know our weaknesses and vulnerabilities but still love us. They are those to whom we have made a gift of ourselves and from whom we have accepted a similar gift. Pseudo-friendship reduces us to our common denominators because it tends to simplify, to encage our personalities in a few surface traits. True friendship diversifies because it discovers and delights in the real complexity of human personhood. It gives us an intimate look into the soul of another and at the same time allows us to see our own soul in another's eyes.

GUIDELINES FOR FRIENDSHIP

Friendships are like houseplants. They need nourishment, sunshine, and conversation. Here are some practical guidelines to help keep your friendships healthy.

GUIDELINE #1

Feed your friendship large doses of constancy, loyalty, and trustworthiness. Let these permeate the soil where it grows.

> *Do not devise harm against your neighbor while he lives in security beside you (3:29).*

> *A friend loves at all times, and a brother is born for adversity (17:17).*

> *A man of many friends comes to ruin, but there is a friend who sticks closer than a brother (18:24).*

> *Do not forsake your own friend or your father's friend, and do not go to your brother's house in the day of your calamity; better is a neighbor who is near than a brother far away (27:10).*

GUIDELINE #2

Prune your friendship as needed by lovingly telling the truth that hurts.

> *A man who flatters his neighbor is spreading a net for his steps (29:5).*

He who rebukes a man will afterward find more favor than he who flatters with the tongue (28:23).

Better is open rebuke than love that is concealed. Faithful are the wounds of a friend, but deceitful are the kisses of an enemy (27:5–6).

GUIDELINE #3
Never pry open the delicate buds of a friend's private life. Let them open of their own accord.

The heart knows its own bitterness, and a stranger does not share its joy (14:10).

Like one who takes a dog by the ears is he who passes by and meddles with strife not belonging to him (26:17).

GUIDELINE #4
Too much harsh sunlight will kill flowering friendships.

A fool always loses his temper, but a wise man holds it back (29:11).

A man's discretion makes him slow to anger, and it is his glory to overlook a transgression (19:11).

He who is slow to anger has great understanding, but he who is quick-tempered exalts folly (14:29).

GUIDELINE #5
Keep the air clean and fresh for the best results.

Keeping away from strife is an honor for a man, but any fool will quarrel (20:3).

It is better to live in a desert land, than with a contentious and vexing woman (21:19).

A brother offended is harder to be won than a strong city, and contentions are like the bars of a castle (18:19).

GUIDELINE #6
Never transplant indiscriminately.

He who goes about as a slanderer reveals secrets, therefore do not associate with a gossip (20:19).

7. Wisdom and the Open-Handed Way to Wealth

Mason was always a hard worker. He started selling firewood from his dad's woods when he was in sixth grade. It was tough work, ferreting out the fallen trees that still held enough wood to be chopped and sold. Over the years he built up a solid clientele that kept him in orders. More than once he had to turn down party invitations during junior high to supply his regular customers. The hours of felling, sawing, chopping, and delivering wood hardened his body and instilled in Mason a love of work and the outdoors. By the time he got to high school, he was managing his own small but successful business, putting in long hours chopping wood, and still managing to keep his grades high enough to run track.

When graduation rolled around, Mason had branched out into some small landscaping jobs. A contractor friend of the family saw his work and offered to let him landscape the grounds of a couple of new houses. Those jobs brought in some regular contracts. By the time Mason's friends were on their way off to college in cars their dads had given them, Mason was investing in his own landscaping equipment and hiring a couple of hands. Within a year, his new venture was off the ground and well on its way to financial success.

Mason enjoyed the creativity of his work as much as the feel of the soil on his fingers and the sun on his back. He took special pride in his work not only because he felt it was his means of improving his neighborhood, but because he also believed his work was his field of service to God. Mason did every landscaping job as though Christ Himself were going to take up residence in the new building.

Unwilling to give up a college education, he enrolled in the local community college. Jobs were delegated and schedules juggled so he could take a degree in a field related to his work. Along the way, Mason fell in love with a girl from his church's young-adult group. They were married and in time, started a family. At thirty, Mason was president of his own successful nursery/landscaping business, a respected leader in his church, a faithful supporter of several missionaries, and a conscientious tither. He found his company's success rewarding, but what he still liked best was the feeling he had driving home after a full day's work with soil under his nails, the smell of fresh air still on his face, and the lingering warmth of the sun on his neck.

Only one thing bothered him. How was he supposed to feel in his heart about his financial success? He had never set out just to see how much money he could make. He just wanted a job and had worked hard at each one. The money seemed to have come almost by itself. But now, what was he to think of it all? Didn't the Bible say the love of money was a root of evil? He had to admit he enjoyed the things his money allowed him to have and to do. Weren't lots of books and preachers saying how immoral it was for Americans to be so rich while others in the world were so poor? What was he to do with his financial prosperity? Should he even be wealthy at all? Maybe he should do as he had heard one speaker advocate—become poor for Jesus. Mason often wrestled with these questions, searching honestly and diligently for biblical answers.

And Mason isn't alone. There's a lot of discussion

today about this problem with different conclusions being drawn. What is the biblical perspective on wealth? Some feel a rich Christian is a contradiction in terms; others teach that a poor Christian is equally a contradiction. One force pulls in the direction of voluntary poverty (at least simplicity of lifestyle) by telling us to devote ourselves to pursuits that do not bring wealth or by divesting ourselves of the wealth we may accumulate. The other force wants us to believe that God has great riches in store for anyone who will serve Him rightly. A great effort is made, on the one hand, to make the Christians of rich, developed countries feel guilty for their wealth in hopes that they will thus be more willing to share it. On the other hand, an effort is made to justify wealth and thus to enjoy its benefits without having to deal with guilt-producing visions of the world's poverty. Generally, this is a volatile issue, which always touches the emotions. As the old saying goes, you can preach to a man all you want without offending him as long as you stay away from his children and his money.

In this chapter, I am going to risk talking about money. For us, Solomon's teachings will be helpful, especially his view of possessions. Wisdom makes a profound impact on our orientation toward possessions. To formulate our stand on wealth without consulting Solomon would be to assure an incomplete view. Let's examine the view of wealth that wisdom engenders. Although we can't say that wealth will necessarily be a by-product of wisdom, we can say that wisdom gives us the correct perspective on wealth. By forming a person's character, wisdom produces the conditions under which wealth may be handled in a healthy, spiritually sound manner.

Wisdom, as expounded in Proverbs, shows four major ideas relating to wealth, which we will examine one by one. Solomon shows us an overview of the relative worth of wealth. He warns against its inherent dangers. He advocates the specific virtues of diligence, frugality, and productivity. And, he makes abundantly clear the responsibility of the wealthy for the poor.

WEALTH IS A QUALIFIED GOOD

Only one conclusion seems possible based on the evidence in Proverbs. Wealth is a qualified good, but not in a moral sense, since possessions are only indirectly moral or immoral. They do, however, have an impact on the life of an individual. In a practical sense, wealth is viewed as a useful, enjoyable facet of life. To be sure, it is not as valuable as some other things. Neither is it without its own quite serious pitfalls. Generally, wealth is not viewed as being evil or shameful. The man of God who walks according to wisdom may or may not be rich, but he will never repudiate wealth as being ungodly.

Several verses in Proverbs show the value of wealth.

> *The rich man's wealth is his fortress, the ruin of the poor is their poverty (10:15).*

> *The wealth of the wise is their crown, but the folly of fools yields folly (14:24 NIV).*

> *The rich rule over the poor, and the borrower becomes the lender's slave (22:7).*

In Proverbs 31, we see a portrait of a "worthy woman," painted with direct and indirect references to her business acumen. She is hard working and possesses no small degree of entrepreneurial know-how. I quote this description at length because it reflects so clearly Proverbs' view of the value of possessions (not to mention the skills that produce it).

> *A wife of noble character . . . is worth far more than rubies. Her husband has full confidence in her and lacks nothing of value. . . . She selects wool and flax and works with eager hands. She is like the merchant ships, bringing her food from afar. She gets up while it is still dark; she provides food for her family and*

> *portions for her servant girls. She considers a field and buys it; out of her earnings she plants a vineyard. She sets about her work vigorously; her arms are strong for her tasks. She sees that her trading is profitable, and her lamp does not go out at night. In her hand she holds the distaff and grasps the spindle with her fingers. She opens her arms to the poor and extends her hands to the needy. When it snows, she has no fear for her household; for all of them are clothed in scarlet. She makes coverings for her bed; she is clothed in fine linen and purple. Her husband is respected at the city gate, where he takes his seat among the elders of the land. She makes linen garments and sells them, and supplies the merchants with sashes. She is clothed with strength and dignity; she can laugh at the days to come. She speaks with wisdom, and faithful instruction is on her tongue. She watches over the affairs of her household and does not eat the bread of idleness (31:10–27 NIV).*

Here is a summary of Proverbs' view of the interplay between wealth, diligence, and wisdom. Solomon often contrasts the harlot and wisdom personified. The "strange woman," as the harlot is usually called, destroys the lives of her lovers; Wisdom builds them up. The harlot takes away; Wisdom gives. Thus, there is a special significance in Proverbs' ending with this lengthy, detailed description of the worthy woman. Here in closing, we have the embodiment of a theme Solomon has been weaving through the entire book. Look at the last two verses, which are particularly revealing. "Charm is deceptive and beauty is fleeting; but a woman *who fears the Lord* is to be praised [a restatement of the book's central theme first given in 1:7]. Give her the reward she has earned, and let her works bring her praise at the city gate" (31:30–31).

For our topic, the overwhelming weight of imagery dealing with diligence, productivity, and wealth is no accident. This imagery is an expression of the ideas scattered liberally throughout Proverbs. Wisdom produces a well-balanced, orderly life, where wealth can be a natural, healthy, useful product. Solomon often contrasts the wise who lead productive lives and the foolish who lead lazy, poverty-stricken lives.

Consider these statements.

> *In the view of Proverbs, a productive life is an asset to be commended as the way for the upright, while laziness is a liability to be despised. Diligence in satisfying life's primary physical needs may bring legitimate wealth and prosperity, while laziness, which leads to poverty and want, is a senseless path to drift along.*[1]

> *Wealth is a source of power, giving economic mastery (13:8, 22:7), while poverty very easily leaves one at the mercy of every upheaval (10:15).*[2]

Proverbs is well aware of the temptations wealth brings. We do not find in it any justification of a selfish, self-satisfied, oppressive way of life. Kindness and generosity are rules rigidly upheld. Yet in spite of these things, wealth is considered to be of genuine value as long as it is rightly treated. "Wealth of itself is neither good nor evil; it is men's use or misuse of it that turns wealth into a blessing or a curse (cf. 10:16)."[3]

Solomon does not hesitate to assure us that living according to wisdom brings circumstances where wealth may be produced. As we have seen in Proverbs 3:9–10, Solomon makes a definitive statement about the relationship between obedience to God and material regards. "Honor the Lord . . . then your barns will be filled to overflowing, and your vats will brim over with new wine." It is, of course, possible to spiritualize this promise by saying that what Solomon really means is honoring God produces emotional stability, inner peace, joy, and so forth. But other verses tell us about the spiritual benefits of wisdom without using the imagery of material wealth. Therefore, I believe Solomon wants to establish clearly the material rewards of serving God. Honoring Him brings material reward. And I believe, as is the nature of all proverbs, this one must be recognized as a general principle of human life, not necessarily a rule that allows no exceptions.

It is not necessary for us to interpret Solomon's references to wealth in spiritualized terms. True, they may make statements about spiritual truths, but it seems clear that Solomon believed and wanted to teach a specific principle, namely, that life lived according to wisdom is a life that stands to benefit materially.

When we read verses like these, we must take them at face value.

> *I walk in the way of righteousness, along the paths of justice, to endow those who love me with wealth, that I may fill their treasuries (8:20–21).*

> *The wicked desires the booty of evil men, but the root of the righteous yields fruit (12:12).*

> *Adversity pursues sinners, but the righteous will be rewarded with prosperity (13:21).*

> *A good man leaves an inheritance to his children's children, and the wealth of the sinner is stored up for the righteous (13:22).*

> *Much wealth is in the house of the righteous, but trouble is in the income of the wicked (15:6).*

> *The reward of humility and the fear of the Lord are riches, honor, and life (22:4).*

> *By wisdom a house is built, and by understanding it is established; and by knowledge the rooms are filled with all precious and pleasant riches (24:3–4).*

Here we need to clarify that Solomon is not teaching us that our riches (or lack of them) are a gauge of wisdom (hence of our spiritual maturity). Neither is he stating an unequivocal fact that all wise people in time become rich people. Instead, he recognizes and verbalizes this principle, which has generally held true in human experience: Obeying God brings material benefit.

Another important aspect of Solomon's overview of wealth must now be put in perspective. We have seen that Solomon believed wealth could be a legitimate, enjoyable circumstance of life and that he saw a general principle connecting wisdom and wealth. But he did not believe material wealth was wisdom's most valuable contribution to life.

Part of our difficulty today in coming to grips with wealth is the false sense of relative worth our age assigns it. Almost without exception, we tend to look upon the pursuit of riches as one of life's most important concerns because it is all but impossible to exist without money. Given the fact that money is so necessary and given our natural state of self-reliance, we can easily see why wealth has such value.

All of these factors except one remain true for the person who lives according to wisdom. He knows that money is necessary for life; he knows that money can be a source of enjoyment; and he knows that wealth unlocks many doors. But he also knows that existence does not have to be a matter of self-reliance. Even more importantly, he knows that satisfaction and enjoyment of life are not really products of wealth. Knowing this, he has committed himself to God-reliance. He trusts in the Creator and has received His assurance that all his needs will be provided for. Thus, he is free to assign to wealth its proper value. It is no longer that which he cannot survive without, that to which he must bend his best efforts to achieve. Wealth becomes simply one of life's variables to be taken in stride.

The only way we will be able to assign to wealth its proper value is by coming to an experiential understanding of what it means to live for God. This is what Solomon wishes to teach us. He states clearly that wealth, though perfectly legitimate and enjoyable, is in no way equal to the spiritual fruits of wisdom.

> *How blessed is the man who finds wisdom, and the man who gains understanding. For its profit is better than the profit of silver, and its gain than fine gold (3:13–14).*

> *Take my instruction, and not silver, and knowledge*
> *rather than choicest gold. For wisdom is better than*
> *jewels; and all desirable things can not compare with*
> *her (8:10–11).*
>
> *There is gold, and an abundance of jewels; but the lips*
> *of knowledge are a more precious thing (20:15).*

For Solomon, wealth was okay. By serving God, he felt everyone had a chance of gaining financially. But more than material wealth, he valued fellowship with his God whereby he received not only wealth, but a long, full life, honor among his peers, pleasantness, joy, understanding, security, freedom from fear, and peace (3:13). Solomon had a healthy, well-balanced view of wealth.

WEALTH'S TEMPTATIONS

The balance of Solomon's view is due in part to his clear-eyed recognition of the dangers wealth brings with it. Riches seem to feed a self-centered, greedy way of life, separating us from godliness unless our hearts are well-founded in wisdom. Solomon tells us that wealth by itself will never give satisfaction and shows us the illegitimate means of accumulating it. Understanding these factors is the next step in our study of wealth.

Anyone who has had even a passing acquaintance with the church, or with the Bible, has heard that some connection exists between money and evil. Unfortunately, that connection is often fuzzy. We know that loving money is supposed to be one of the all-star sins. But when it comes to a distinct understanding of what the Bible really teaches, we are at a loss. By immersing ourselves in the Book of Proverbs, we see four temptations that the wealthy will have to battle.

First, as our riches increase, we will have to fight the temptation to put our trust in them instead of God.

> *He who trusts in his riches will fall, but the righteous*
> *will flourish like the green leaf (11:28).*

Of course, it is entirely possible for a poor man to look to money as his salvation. But when you possess wealth, the temptation is even greater to believe it can answer all questions, provide for all needs, and assure satisfaction. It can't. The only thing that can be such a source of security and satisfaction in this life is righteousness—a living relationship with the Creator. While wealth can be a useful tool and provide for much enjoyment of the things with which God has filled our world, it can never be that inner source of strength, which animates a life like sap does a tree. A growing love for our Lord must continually flow in us, renewing our strength and bearing precious fruit. Our trust must never be taken from Him and placed in a substitute.

A second temptation is to believe that riches insulate us from the experiences of life common to all men.

> *A rich man's wealth is his strong city, And like a high wall in his own imagination (18:11).*

A rich man's wealth tends to become a fantasy, spinning webs of false security and insulation from all that the poor folk outside his fortress must face. Locked in his castle with the drawbridge pulled up and sentries on the wall, the rich man looks out on life and says, "I am different. I am not like those slaving folk down in the valley. I have influence; I have power; I command respect. I cannot be touched by tragedy."

Creeping into the rich man's castle like a fog and breaking his heart, Sorrow knows no walls. All of us, rich and poor alike, breathe God's air, enjoy His sun, and eat the fruit of the earth He has given us. The laws of human life, though they may be masked for a time by wealth, can never be transcended by it. In the end, wealth will prove itself to be the shimmering mirage that it always was. The poor rich man will see his vulnerability.

How much better to pursue the course of righteousness. "The name of the Lord is a strong tower; the righteous runs into it and is safe" (18:10).

A third temptation is allowing the pursuit of riches to become a consuming passion, which wears away life and eventually betrays the effort it has demanded.

> *Do not weary yourself to gain wealth, cease from your consideration of it. When you set your eyes on it, it is gone. For wealth certainly makes itself wings, like an eagle that flies toward the heavens (23:4–5).*

A well-known phenomenon is that we never seem to have enough money. If we earn $12,000 a year, we feel that life would just be bearable if we earned $15,000. If we earn $50,000 a year, we see how much better $75,000 would be. One level raises us just high enough to see and desire the next. This is a wearying, endless cycle, which, left unchecked, can drain away life's vitality. Worst of all, this mistaken view of wealth fixes our eyes on what does not possess the advertised goods. More money does not necessarily guarantee a better life. The only thing more money really guarantees is the necessity to spend more trying to find out how to pay less in taxes.

Solomon says that no one ought to spend his life pursuing wealth. First, wealth, as an end in itself, allows for no satisfaction. The richest miser always dreams of having more. Further, wealth is patently unstable. If we spend our lives to accumulate it, we will have spent our lives for something that can leave us overnight. "When you set your eyes on it, it is gone. For wealth certainly makes itself wings." The best investment plans or the most secure financial arrangements cannot alter the basically unstable nature of riches.

Allowing wealth to become a consuming goal is the temptation we face. I am always saddened to hear someone say, "My goal is to earn $100,000 a year by the time I'm thirty-five." Such a person is consumed by the temptation to hold wealth in the wrong priority. He assures for himself a lifetime of unfulfilled dreams unless somehow his priorities get rearranged.

Solomon's idea is sounder. Focus on maintaining a diligent, careful lifestyle. Hold in your heart the things that make life truly happy. Conduct your business as a service to those about you as efficiently, and as profitably, as you honestly can. If all that results in riches, be thankful for the wealth. But never, never let the pursuit of wealth enslave you.

The fourth temptation is the tendency of wealth to dull our moral sensitivity.

> *The righteousness of the upright will deliver them, but the treacherous will be caught by their own greed (11:6).*
>
> *A man with an evil eye hastens after wealth, and does not know that want will come upon him (28:22).*

Covetousness becomes an engulfing evil; avariciousness acts as a poison to moral values. Therefore, wealth brings with it the temptation to turn a blind eye to injustice and immorality. Everything is capable of being rationalized into innocence when the pursuit of greater wealth is at stake. In this sense, wealth can have a tendency to degrade those it owns. When we turn away from justice in the pursuit of wealth, we insure to ourselves want. Someone with an evil eye whose heart is filled with lust for material wealth does not even realize that greed is eating away at the core of his soul. One day he will awaken to see he is a shell encased in rubies, a corpse covered in diamonds.

How much better to serve God than riches! How much better to love people, to laugh with the rippling brooks and breathe the rhythm of the sighing pines, to share secrets with a playing squirrel and spirit-soar with the eagles than to be trapped by the musty, artificial clank of coined gods! The simple but majestic joys of daily life are what we are made for. But the perversion of Satan's work turns our hearts from God to ourselves. Ultimately, to love money is to love self. Against this central temptation of wealth stands the clear, piercing call of the Lord.

The fear of the Lord leads to life: Then one rests content (19:23 NIV).

Never, until then!

THE VALUE OF DILIGENCE

Where has our study led us? We have seen Solomon's view of the value of wealth, as well as its dangers. We know that he believed wealth, rightly regarded, to be a useful, enjoyable possibility. He has taught us that wealth is not evil but can be a tool of righteousness. There is no shame in a godly man's wealth. Rather, wealth is to be enjoyed and used responsibly, guarding against the serious pitfalls it carries. Here I may add that wealth is no more dangerous to godly living than the temptation to sexual immorality, for example. Both are open to being made perversions of the good things God gives. Finally, we have seen that if we are to be guided by wisdom, we can never make the pursuit of wealth the purpose of our lives.

How then is a godly man to acquire wealth? Must he sit idly waiting for the chances of life to give or deprive him of it? Is wealth or poverty a destiny fixed for individuals by God or circumstances?

Solomon answers these questions unmistakably. Let's summarize again.

(1) Wealth is a qualified good.

(2) Wealth carries with it temptations that must be guarded against.

(3) Wealth must never be our life's goal. . . . *but*

(4) Diligence in the tasks to which we set ourselves coupled with a godly, frugal, generous lifestyle has every likelihood of producing wealth.

Not every godly person will be wealthy because not all godly men wish to be wealthy. On the other hand, when an individual and when a society chooses to govern themselves according to wisdom—when they choose to live in fellowship with God—a general effect will be the rise of material prosperity.

Let's take a look at some of Solomon's words about diligence.

> *Go to the ant, O sluggard, observe her ways and be wise, which, having no chief, officer, or ruler prepares her food in the summer, and gathers her provision in the harvest. How long will you lie down, O sluggard? When will you arise from your sleep? "A little sleep, a little slumber, a little folding of the hands to rest"— and your poverty will come in like a vagabond, and your need like an armed man (6:6–11).*

> *Poor is he who works with a negligent hand, but the hand of the diligent makes rich (10:4).*

> *The hand of the diligent will rule, but the slack hand will be put to forced labor (12:24).*

> *A slothful man does not roast his prey, but the precious possession of a man is diligence (12:27).*

> *The soul of the sluggard craves and gets nothing, but the soul of the diligent is made fat (13:4).*

> *A worker's appetite works for him, for his hunger urges him on (16:26).*

> *He also who is slack in his work is brother to him who destroys (18:9).*

> *Laziness casts into a deep sleep, and an idle man will suffer hunger (19:15).*

> *The sluggard does not plow after the autumn, so he begs during the harvest and has nothing (20:4).*

> *Do not love sleep, lest you become poor; Open your eyes, and you will be satisfied with food (20:13).*

> *Do you see a man skilled in his work? He will stand before kings; he will not stand before obscure men (22:29).*

These are but a sampling of Solomon's recommendations for an industrious way of life. Definite limits are set on the methods by which we may gain wealth. While it is possible to become wealthy through violence of one form or another (11:16), this is obviously not an avenue open to the godly. To profit by illicit acts is to harm oneself (15:27). We are forbidden to profit by any form of injustice (16:8; 22:16). Wealth if gotten with strife is no good (17:1). Any form of dishonesty and robbery of the customer is immoral and prohibited (20:10; 21:6; 28:6). Interest and usury to break the back of the poor are forbidden (28:8).

Nevertheless, we are amply encouraged to conduct our legitimate businesses in a productive manner. Solomon would much rather see the world's wealth in the hands of godly men than in the grasp of sinners. If by hard, honest labor you gain wealth, good! Ask God for help in guarding yourself against the temptations it brings, but by all means, enjoy what God gives you and use it for His glory.

OPEN HEART, OPEN HAND

Now we see the final pillar in Solomon's view of wealth. I have already said our wealth must be used responsibly. Solomon clearly tells us to use it to provide for our families (13:22) and to provide ourselves with precious, pleasant things (24:3–4). But above all, our wealth must be dedicated to the poor and needy about us. Beyond the tithe, we have no specific, across-the-board rule about how much we ought to give. A godly man does not ask himself, *How much must I give?* but *How much can I give?* His is an open hand, giving and then receiving God's blessing for having given. God is never in debt to His children.

Has God allowed you to earn riches? Here's concrete advice what to do with them.

> *Do not withhold good from those to whom it is due, when it is in your power to do it. Do not say to your neighbor, "Go, and come back, and tomorrow I will give it," when you have it with you (3:27–28).*
>
> *There is one who scatters, yet increases all the more, and there is one who withholds what is justly due, but it results only in want. The generous man will be prosper-*

ous, and he who waters will himself be watered (11:24–25).

He who despises his neighbor sins, but happy is he who is gracious to the poor (14:21).

He who is gracious to a poor man lends to the Lord, and He will repay him for his good deed (19:17).

He who shuts his ear to the cry of the poor will also cry himself and not be answered (21:13).

He who is generous will be blessed, for he gives some of his food to the poor (22:9).

He who gives to the poor will never want, but he who shuts his eyes will have many curses (28:27).

Can you look into the pleading eyes of a starving child and then sit down to your abundant meal comfortably? Can you feel the pain of poverty as it grinds the hearts of the disadvantaged and then comfortably buy the latest lavish trinket? It is no consolation to blame the poor for their poverty. We still have this command: "The rich and the poor have a common bond, the Lord is the maker of them all" (22:2).

GUIDELINES FOR GIVING

We are given these practical guidelines for giving.

(1) Give only good. Weigh your gift and the manner in which you intend to give it. Will it result in good for the recipient? If necessary, do some research. Ask questions before you plunge. Is there some better thing you might give, or some better way to give it? In general, give discreetly with no strings attached. Give out of genuine love. Do not give money if you can give yourself.

(2) Give to whom it is due. Learn to discern (by prayer and practice) the prompting of the Holy Spirit about who should receive your gifts. What you have to give is not yours. It is God's and should not be given indiscriminately.

(3) Giving is gaining. What you hoard you can only lose. What you give is an investment in a carefree future.

(4) Giving without graciousness is insulting. Learn to see the place of giving as the place of humility. To be gracious in giving is to be tactful, courteous, and motivated by true kindness. Anything less is a form of bribery.

(5) When you give to the poor, you give to the Lord. When we learn to see in the hand reaching out to receive our gift, the hand of the Lord who gave all that was His for us, we have the proper perspective about giving.

· • ● • ·

In the heart of the Creator, wealth or poverty never colors His love. Each of us was worth dying for. If we are all recipients of such unconditional love, how can we withhold good when we have it to give? Wealth is fine; enjoy it if you have it. But always keep a generous heart and an open hand.

8. Wisdom and the Way We Talk

Have you ever considered the power we hold over people merely in the way we choose to talk to or about them? Words can relieve or exacerbate circumstances, soothe or injure someone. Here's an example.

Chad and Melissa are in their thirties and have one child, a three-year-old son. Both hold down demanding, full-time jobs. Chad's accounting firm requires long hours of tedious, exacting work, which often leaves him mentally and emotionally drained. Melissa directs a nursery school where she takes their son every day. After eight hours of riding herd on three dozen preschoolers, she wants nothing more than to sit down to a quiet meal that someone else has prepared with normal conversation and no spilled milk. Her son Tommy, who has had to share his mommy all day with thirty-five other kids, is ready for some personal attention, whining and sulking if he doesn't get it.

As Chad, Melissa, and Tommy rendezvous around the supper table each evening, the stage is set for some interesting give-and-take. Never underestimate the power of words at moments like these. For purposes of discussion, let's just suppose these folks are especially short-tempered one particular evening and a bit on the insensitive side.

Melissa arrives home from work first with Tommy in tow. She has to tell him repeatedly to, "get out of the car; bring your papers; leave the flowers alone; don't worry about the bug; come on now, you'll be left behind; hurry up Tommy, Mommy's waiting; get in here right now young man!" She throws her things on the coffee table and bone-weary, slumps onto the couch for a few minutes rest before getting supper. She had put a chicken into the crock pot this morning but forgot to turn it on before leaving, so she will have to prepare something else on the spur of the moment. But first, some rest.

Just as her leaden limbs begin to relax, Tommy runs a dump truck, engine roaring, up her right leg and across her tummy.

"Please, Tommy," she pleads, "just let Mommy have a few minutes rest."

She relaxes again but, before she realizes it, has dozed for fifteen minutes. Chad will be home shortly, and supper is still ensconced in the refrigerator in plastic containers. Just as Melissa forces herself to a sitting position, a thunderous crash from the den signals the fact that Tommy has ignored her repeated commands not to climb the bookcase and has succeeded in pulling it over onto himself. He is not seriously hurt but thinks he is and will howl accordingly for many more minutes than Melissa's frayed nerves can stand.

After some comfort for the injured mountain climber (I use the word "comfort" loosely.) and a few hasty efforts to repair the damage, she arrives in the kitchen determined to whip up one of those "Ten Superdelicious Polynesian Feasts Made with Everyday Leftovers" she has recently read about.

Chad stumbles in the front door. Things haven't exactly been straight and level for him all day. His time has been spent with an anxious customer whose tax returns are being audited. Though feeling especially drained, he knows if the yard is not mowed tonight, he will need a map to find the front gate again. The mower wouldn't start last Tuesday when he had planned to mow, so his first order of business should be to change its spark plug and try to coax it to life.

After a quick Hi to Melissa and a nimble dodge of the dump truck careening wildly down the hall, he goes to change his clothes. He will spend the next half-hour wrestling with the perverse lawn mower, taking the skin off of two knuckles, and generously sprinkling himself with oil.

As this lovely, all-American, Christian family sits down for supper, it would be an exaggeration to say they are ready for mutually enriching, stimulating conversation. Chad's first mistake is a sly comment about Polynesian-fried mashed potatoes. Melissa tries ignoring the remark and asks innocently about the health of the lawn mower. Tommy howls for more Polynesian-fried hot dogs. Chad growls about the stuck spark plug and complains about his chain-smoking customer. Melissa observes that he, at least, hasn't had to cope with twenty-four failing candidates for potty training. Unable to resist, Chad wonders out loud what happened to the barbecued chicken that went into the crock pot this morning. Melissa explains somewhat testily that mere humans do forget things now and then. Tommy spills his milk on Chad's lap, and Chad nearly upsets the table trying to get out of the way. Melissa laughs from tension and fatigue and because it didn't happen to her. Chad glowers. Tommy gets some fatherly wisdom on the virtues of paying attention to what he's doing. Melissa observes that it was an accident. Chad stomps off to change his pants. When he gets back, he wonders out loud why Melissa can't be a little more organized. She wonders why Chad can't be a little more understanding. The rest of the evening will be spent trying to think up ways to express their frustration sweetly, without actually being inconsiderate.

Never underestimate the power of words at moments like these! Chad and Melissa have allowed themselves to become victims of their circumstances. They have let their fatigue and tension dictate how they talk to each other, as well as their topics for discussion. Instead of words of kindness and understanding about their respective struggles, they throw at each other words that will only make the problems worse. If they are not careful, damage will be done that even later apologies will not fully undo. The circumstances will pass without a scar; the fatigue and tension can be handled. But the words they exchange will leave lasting impressions.

All of us use words. Sometimes we use them wisely; many times we wield them like dangerous weapons. We have seen what wisdom produces in three specific areas of life: personal righteousness, basic relationships, and possessions. In this chapter, we turn our attention to the use of words. Words are the medium through which human community is formed and maintained, muscular workmen by whom we express ourselves and interact with one another. It should come as no surprise that Solomon was concerned with the way we use words. Proverbs teaches that wisdom makes all the difference in what we choose to say and how we choose to say it. Wisdom dictates increased responsibility for the sentences we set adrift. Words can be missiles with deadly shrapnel to rip and tear, bombs to annihilate those they hit. Or, they can be rivers of clear, soothing water, spices to add flavor to life, medicine to help heal the injuries of those around us. Solomon tells us that adopting wisdom as our life-code is a commitment to the right use of words.

A TALKING GOD

What do we mean by the right use of words? Is there really a right and a wrong way to talk? Aren't words just an innocent part of everyday life?

Without a doubt, they are part of everyday life, but

never innocent. Words are a direct gift from God, that is, we do not have them by chance. True, many of us give very little thought to the thousands of words that slip through our lips in the course of our lives. We think much more often about our health, our earning power, and our physical resources and guard these jealously. According to Solomon, our word resources must be just as jealously guarded, just as wisely used. There is a right and a wrong way to spend this precious commodity. God is vitally interested in what pours from our lips because, like the desire for fellowship, this power of language is an expression of His image in us. Language is not to be taken lightly; talk isn't cheap. Our words can't be thrown around recklessly with no thought given to their conception and results.

Words are an expression of that intangible possession of man, that shimmering reflection in him of the genius of God. Often in our speculating about whether life exists elsewhere in our universe, what we long to know is if *intelligent* life exists. There is a spark of celestial fire— something unique we recognize in ourselves—that is a watershed running through all time and space. On one side lies all of subhuman life, all the magnificent examples of God's creative wealth. On the other lies man, the only creature into which, we are told, God breathed His breath. God put something of Himself into all the orders of creation from the smallest one-celled organism to the mightiest jungle animal. According to His own revelation, He breathed His spirit into only one—man. Intelligence is a fragile word to use in describing the mind of God, but somehow man's intelligence must be that of the mind of God, which was given him in creation. Thus, the use of language—the expression of that intelligence—becomes something of a divine act. In the faculty of speech, we see our parentage. We see that we have come from the one Speaker.

From our very first glimpse of God given, we see

that He is a talking God. In creation, He spoke the world into existence. After He had made man with His hands, He spoke to him. In all God's subsequent self-revelation, He has been speaking to His creatures. He has not simply resorted to cataclysmic events of nature, to omens and signals in the sky. He has talked to us, speaking our language as one person to another. Even when God sent His Son, He was called the Word. Perhaps we have become so familiar with this whole concept of communication by speech that we cannot see how awesome it really is. In their divine origin, however, we find the fundamental reason for the importance and power of words.

WHAT WORDS CAN DO

Solomon shows us three capabilities of speech. First, as we have already hinted, words are the medium through which God has chosen to reveal truth, to teach and counsel wisdom. Solomon invites us to come. Listen to his words.

> *"Let your heart hold fast my words; keep my commandments and live"(4:4).*
>
> *Hear, my son, and accept my sayings (4:10).*
>
> *My son, give attention to my words; incline your ear to my sayings (4:20).*
>
> *Now then, my sons, listen to me, and do not depart from the words of my mouth (5:7).*

Many ways of teaching exist. No matter what method we choose, some idea must be communicated. That idea can be conveyed in words that carry truth. Ideas are not simply airy, ephemeral things that live uselessly in our minds but engines that drive our daily lives. The ideas you imbibe in the words your mind receives don't leave you unchanged. Nothing goes in one ear and out the other. Everything you hear becomes a part of you and, in some small way, changes you forever.

It is for this reason that Solomon was so concerned that we immerse ourselves in wisdom. "Listen to the truth God gives," he counseled, "for only in it do we have something by which to evaluate all the other ideas that will flow into us." Therefore, one of the main capabilities of words, something we must never take lightly, is this ability to communicate ideas. Words mold our lives!

Secondly, Solomon instructs us that how we use words is an expression of our unique character. We wear our words like badges. We reveal the condition of our heart not so much in the specific things we say but in our manner with words, in the *kinds* of things we are apt to say in our unguarded speech. Words are such that we can say just about anything we feel like saying. Reality doesn't necessarily have to back us up. That is why the specific claims a man makes may be an unreliable gauge of what his inner life is really like. However, by listening carefully to the overall way he talks, even to the very words he uses, we can get a pretty accurate picture of what's going on inside him.

The third general observation given about words is that they hold the power of life and death in the human community. As Solomon says,

> *Death and life are in the power of the tongue, And those who love it will eat its fruit (18:21).*

Words are far from impotent among people. Not only can we snare our own lives by our words but we can also make or break others by the way we talk to or about them. Let's illustrate these briefly.

Solomon, speaking in the context of unwisely going surety for someone else's loan, says,

> *If you have been snared with the words of your mouth, have been caught with the words of your mouth, do this then, my son, and deliver yourself (6:2–3).*

Rash promises are a snare to an honest man because he is bound by conscience to keep them. When we give our word, it's as if we have signed a contract. Further, by taking a stand before knowing the issues at stake or by giving our answer before hearing the entire question, we lay traps for ourselves. Solomon cautions us that words are not to be taken lightly. When we speak, we need to be aware of the importance and lasting repercussions our words make.

Of course, little illustration is needed to remind us of the power words have over the lives of others. A habit we would do well to cultivate is to guard doubly carefully even the most innocent things we say about others. Even then, we may be guilty of coloring another's reputation, but we will be extremely sensitive to this possibility and do all we can to guard against it.

Let's suppose, for instance, that you are a long-standing member of a certain church or a longtime employee of a business. With ample opportunity, you have formed impressions of the people around you.

Let's say a new person comes into the church or is hired by your firm. As that new individual begins to move in your familiar circles, he will be going through the process of forming his own impressions. Most importantly, he will be extremely susceptible to the opinions of his new peers. Even though he may not accept them as his own, he cannot help being influenced by them. He is, after all, in new circumstances and is taking in all the information he can get. As he makes acquaintances, the words you say, even the most innocent expression, will carry weight. If you express your views about someone you happen to dislike, you will color the new person's relationship with him. He will be less able to form his own opinions if he has to work through yours, too. Unfortunately, it often seems our favorite pastime to take the new person aside for a few "kindly words of advice" about dealing with so-and-so. This is an injustice not only to the person about whom you are speaking but also to the person to whom you speak.

Words have the power of life and death. We are horrified when we read about brutal, senseless murders. We are disgusted and saddened when a rape takes place. We shrink from the indiscriminate carnage of war. Why, then, do we casually murder with words? We can utterly destroy one person in the eyes of another by a knowing smirk here and a deft jibe there. We can rape them by taking their secrets and spreading them to the winds. Some of us have been at war for years using words instead of guns, but inflicting pain and damage just the same. For all of these acts, we will be held accountable. Words are not cheap, but ever so costly. One of wisdom's by-products is an increased awareness of this power and a heightened sensitivity about how we use it.

There are four specific styles of speech reflected in Proverbs. These may be habitual patterns or used only as they serve our purposes. Three of them fall far short of wisdom's way; however, the fourth is emphasized for our pattern. I have given them four titles: the adulterous way with words, the foolish way with words, the treacherous way with words, and the wise way with words. Although these are not titled exactly this way in Proverbs, they are clearly depicted there.

As we take the material Solomon gives to pencil composite sketches, give some thought to your own way of talking. Which style do you use? Perhaps yours is a mix of the four? Where might wisdom need to reform your ways with words?

The Adulterous Way with Words

You may recall that Solomon often contrasts wisdom with the adulteress. He spends much time warning his listeners to stay away from the harlot, who will eventually be a source of great pain. She characteristically uses words as velvety enticements, which conceal a hidden sting. Although Solomon describes a harlot here, anyone can speak this same way. You might agree with me that it

117

appears Madison Avenue has taken its current sales tricks right out of the adulteress' mouth. Here is Solomon's picture.

The words of the adulteress are smooth and honey-coated. She is stylish, knows all the latest jargon, and can match wits with anyone. This outward smoothness masks an inner lack of sincerity and a plethora of ulterior motives.

> *My Son, give attention to my wisdom, incline your ear to my understanding; that you may observe discretion, and your lips may reserve knowledge. For the lips of an adulteress drip honey, and smoother than oil is her speech; but in the end she is bitter as wormwood, sharp as a two-edged sword (5:1–4).*

She makes frequent use of flattery, trying with heartless compliments to extract something from rather than build up her listener.

> *The foreigner [adulteress] . . . flatters with her words (7:5).*
>
> *With her flattering lips she seduces (7:21).*

She is full of persuasions to bring her listener around to her point of view, to draw him into her foolish ways.

> *With her many persuasions she entices him (7:21).*

Look at the kinds of things she uses to persuade her listener. She attempts to give her arguments legitimacy by referring to her good actions: "I was due to offer peace offerings; today I have paid my vows" (7:14). She tries to make her listener feel as though he is the most important person in the world, even though she is entirely insincere: "Therefore I have come out to meet *you*, to seek *your* presence earnestly, and I have found you" (7:15). She spins castles of sensuous pleasure in the air: "I have sprinkled my bed with myrrh, aloes and cinnamon" (7:16). She plays on her listener's legitimate desires: "Come, let us drink our fill of love until morning; let us delight ourselves with caresses" (7:18). She offers glib assurances of complete safety: "The man is not at home, he has gone on a long journey; he has taken a bag of money with him, at full moon he will come home" (7:19–20).

This, then, is one way we may use words. We may be smooth and attractive with many arguments to persuade our listeners and get what we want; however, we are insincere, not caring so much about our listeners as we do about our personal interests. As a result of our being less than wholesome and forthright, people will gain nothing but skepticism by contact with us.

The Foolish Way with Words

Another style of speech is that of the fool. In Proverbs, we find the portrayal of the person who indulges in light, giddy, empty conversation, frittering away the time with useless, banal observations. His talk reflects a heart full of transient interests, attached to nothing of substance. Here's Solomon's characterization of him.

The fool finds himself snared with his own words. Since he pays little attention to what he says, he is apt to make careless promises, which he will later regret.

> *If you have been snared with the words of your mouth
> . . . deliver yourself (6:2).*

He babbles endlessly about anything that happens to come into his mind or across his field of vision. Thus, he is often seen with his foot in his mouth, going from one scrape into another.

> *A babbling fool will be thrown down (10:8).*
>
> *When there are many words, transgression is unavoidable, but he who restrains his lips is wise (10:19).*
>
> *The one who opens wide his lips comes to ruin (13:3).*

He has no discretion about the repetition of private matters, so he is an incurable gossip. Nothing is safe with him.

> *A prudent man conceals knowledge, but the heart of*
> *fools proclaims folly (12:23).*

His words, rather than supporting and disseminating knowledge, are busy spouting off the latest speculative foolishness.

> *The tongue of the wise makes knowledge acceptable,*
> *but the mouth of fools spouts folly (15:2).*
>
> *The lips of the wise spread knowledge, but the hearts of*
> *fools are not so (15:7).*

He is not in the habit of waiting until he understands the issues involved in a controversy before blazing away with his answer.

> *He who gives an answer before he hears, it is folly and*
> *shame to him (18:13).*

He is one of the loudest mockers of true wisdom. He can "see through" anything, knowing where he stands and having no time for those who do not agree with him instantly and completely.

> *Do not speak in the hearing of a fool, for he will despise*
> *the wisdom of your words (23:9).*

When the fool does happen upon some truth, he renders it utterly useless (even dangerous) with his lame application of it.

> *Like the legs which hang down from the lame, so is a*
> *proverb in the mouth of fools (26:7).*
>
> *Like a thornbush which falls into the hand of a*
> *drunkard, so is a proverb in the mouth of fools (26:9).*

Do you know anyone like this? Unfortunately, all of us seem bent on playing the fool from time to time. But as they say, forewarned is forearmed.

The Treacherous Way with Words

A third way with words is that of the treacherous. Where the adulteress is smooth and well-oiled with the hope of gaining her ulterior motive; where the fool is empty and giddy, the treacherous are violent. They are those who take pleasure in cutting others down to size, wielding words meanly, desiring to hurt, deceive, and destroy.

The treacherous are given to falsehood.

> *A lying tongue hates those it crushes, and a flattering mouth works ruin (26:28).*

They conceal, yet perpetrate violence. Their words destroy those who live trustingly around them.

> *The mouth of the wicked conceals violence (10:11).*
>
> *With his mouth the godless man destroys his neighbor (11:9).*
>
> *The desire of the treacherous is violence (13:2).*

Their words are rash and quick. Harshly, they give no thought to the damage they may do nor to the hurt they may cause, like a scorching fire.

> *There is one who speaks rashly like the thrusts of a sword, but the tongue of the wise brings healing (12:18).*
>
> *A worthless man digs up evil, while his words are as a scorching fire (16:27).*

They pervert the truth, twisting things until they are false and stirring up enmity and confusion.

> *A soothing tongue is a tree of life, but perversion in it crushes the spirit (15:4).*

They are whisperers, spreading malicious rumors that keep debate riled up to add flame to the fire.

> *For lack of wood the fire goes out, and where there is no whisperer, contention quiets down (26:20).*
>
> *The words of a whisperer are like dainty morsels, and they go down into the innermost parts of the body (26:22).*

The adulteress is a trap; the fool, a waste of time; and the treacherous, a hostile enemy. Of these three, the treacherous inflict the most pain. We would do well to make sure we never, ever indulge in the destructive ways of the treacherous.

The Wise Way with Words

Finally, we come to the one way given as a model to imitate. Most of us would probably have to admit we have used the other three from time to time; one of them may even have become habitual. Of course, we must recognize that there is a time for persuasion if it is honest and sincere, a time for levity if it is not abused. However, if we have let our speech be dominated by these other styles, we need to pay careful attention to what Solomon teaches about the wise way with words.

Solomon says that the man who lives according to wisdom is unquestionably honest. He is as good as his word.

> *Put away from you a deceitful mouth, and put devious*
> *lips far from you (4:24).*

His speech is populated by upright ideas and sentiments, so his conversation is not only interesting but also edifying.

> *Listen, for I shall speak noble things; and the opening*
> *of my lips will produce right things (8:6).*
> *The tongue of the wise makes knowledge acceptable*
> *(15:2).*

He keeps to himself those things shared in confidence. For this reason, he is often a trusted counselor. People know they are safe with him.

> *He who goes about as a talebearer reveals secrets, but*
> *he who is trustworthy conceals a matter (11:13).*

When the occasion calls for it, he is ready with advice and encouragement. His is "a word of friendly encouragement from a sympathizing heart [that] cheers the sorrowful soul, and, if only for a time, changes its sorrow into the joy of confidence and of hope!"[1]

> *Anxiety in the heart of a man weighs it down, but a good word makes it glad (12:25).*

A wise man knows how to offer insight into the circumstances at hand. His answers hit the nail on the head. People depend on his advice.

> *A man has joy in an apt answer, and how delightful is a timely word! (15:23).*

> *Like apples of gold in settings of silver is a word spoken in right circumstances (25:11).*

Unlike the babbling fool, the wise man gives much thought to his speech. His conversation comes from a deep inner well of personal study and reflection. Thus, it contains well-thought out ideas and matters of real substance. The wisdom that characterizes his life shows in his speech.

> *The heart of the righteous ponders how to answer, but the mouth of the wicked pours out evil things (15:28).*

> *The wise in heart will be called discerning, and sweetness of speech increases persuasiveness (16:21).*

> *The heart of the wise teaches his mouth, and adds persuasiveness to his lips (16:23).*

Rather than using words to return hostilities, rather than trying to bulldoze his own views with strong words, the wise man has mastered the art of the gentle answer. But he does not put stinging meaning into velveted sentences, instead he responds with words that heal and soothe. "The soft tongue is the opposite of a passionate, sharp, coarse one, which only the more increases the resistance which it seeks to overcome. . . . Cutting, immoderate language embitters and drives away; gentle words, on the contrary, persuade.[2]

> *A gentle answer turns away wrath, but a harsh word stirs up anger (15:1).*

> *By forbearance a ruler may be persuaded, and a soft tongue breaks the bone (25:15).*

The wise man exercises restraint in his speech. He feels no desperate compulsion to add his views to every discussion. For this reason, his views carry more weight when they are heard.

He who restrains his words has knowledge, and he who has a cool spirit is a man of understanding (17:27).

He who guards his mouth and his tongue, guards his soul from troubles (21:23).

If we were to use Solomon's portrait of the wise way with words, the world would be a much less hazardous, much more orderly place! Our speech, if we adopt wisdom's way, will not always be perfect. We will stumble from time to time. We won't always have an apt answer. Still, allowing wisdom to mold our patterns of speech helps us to avoid the other styles that certainly will come to no good end.

In the final analysis, our words are nothing more than a public expression of our inner life. By our actions and by our words, we show who we are. If our hearts are full of anger and bitterness, our words will be cruel and sharp edged. If our minds have not been stoked with truth and wisdom, our mouths will find nothing edifying to say. If our affections are twisted and perverted by sin, our tongue will spill out poisoned foolishness. On the other hand, when we have consciously chosen to put our lives under the direction of God's will and are consistently doing all we can to learn and live by that will, our conversation will take on the tone of wisdom.

Believe me, this is not just lofty theorizing! It is a practical reality. Try listening to the people around you for a while—I mean really listening. Listen behind their words; probe their public thoughts. Try to uncover what their hearts are attached to. Before long, you will be surprised how clearly you can tell the myriads of ideas, affections, hurts, and axes to grind that motivate the conversations around you.

Cultivating a Wise Way with Words

Solomon's teaching gives us guidelines—not necessarily steps to better speech—but truths to remember as you learn.

Our way with words is something we have developed over a lifetime. Anyone reading this book has had years to build present speech habits that will not change overnight. They can, however, be modified and eventually rebuilt with some consistent effort. To that end, a helpful project might be to evaluate the way we use words. How much time do you spend complaining? How often do you give in to the temptation to attack people unlovingly and unfairly? How often does your conversation contribute something really useful to the situation? Try coming to a clear idea of your habitual way with words.

Taking the guidelines listed below, devote conscious, consistent practice to them. Spend some time on each one asking God to show you your areas of need. If some area arises where you have special difficulty, devote an extra day to it. Don't expect your way with words to change radically in a week. Instead, devote your time to looking for areas of strength or weakness. Are you good at giving complimentary, affirming words? Do you have a problem with honesty? After some time spent doing this, you will be well on your way to tightening up your conversational habits. Words aren't easy to control. Used rightly though, they can be rewarding tools of friendship and healing.

(1) Allow God to mold your tongue. When you become aware of a problem area, such as honesty, vulgarity, backbiting, present it to Him and ask for guidance to improve. (See 16:1.)

(2) Consciously cultivate rigorous honesty. As Solomon says again and again, falsehood is *never* the better way! Total honesty is hard. We love to weasel our way out of the truth when it looks threatening or painful. Don't let yourself off the hook! (See 4:24; 6:12–19; 12:19, 22; 13:5.)

(3) Learn the art of the gentle answer. Try to discern the condition of your listener's heart and look for what motivates his words. Evaluate rather than react. At all times, let love and understanding temper what you say. (See 12:25; 15:1; 16:21; 25:15.)

(4) Speak from your heart. Let your private reflection on God's truth produce the substance of your words. Always be sincere and ready to stand behind what you say. (See 15:28; 16:23.)

(5) Guard against using words destructively. Resist all temptation to slander, respecting other people's private lives. Weigh your words according to their motivation and their effect. Murder with words can be just as real as murder with a gun. (See 10:18; 11:13; 12:18, 23; 16:27; 25:23.)

(6) When you can, be quiet. (See 17:28.)

9. When Wisdom Wins

What are the processes by which life-codes may be changed? How do we pull ourselves away from modes of thought and action that have become normal? Is it possible to put new ones in their place?

In speaking of changing life-codes, we must consciously broaden our discussion to include concepts foreshadowed in Solomon but never brought to full disclosure until the ministry of Christ. These are the concepts of faith in Christ and of conversion. For those of us living today, faith in Christ that transforms our lives is the beginning of wisdom. While Solomon intimates these ideas often, they only find complete expression in the person and work of Jesus Christ. The transformation Christ makes is the foundation on which the biblical life-code is built. Many have never experienced this transformation of heart in spite of prolonged attempts to live a worthy life. My hope for them is that they will take this first step that leads to true wisdom. Those who have committed their lives to Christ will be ready to press on in the quest of a biblical life-code. Proverbs can encourage them to let every area of their lives come under the direction of the Word and will of God and to know the fulfillment of having a well-formed, functioning biblical life-code. Building wisdom is a lifelong pursuit, the end of which not even the saintliest can boast of having seen. But the more we strive to learn, the more we have to practice. And the more we practice, the more we see the satisfaction of living our lives for God. May wisdom win your heart!

THE HEART, LIFE'S SEED

My oldest daughter shares my love of books. Nothing makes her happier than rummaging through the library for two or three new ones to read. One of our pleasures is curling up together after supper in a chair with some good stories. It's something we both enjoy doing and is a good way to spend time together.

Not long ago, she and I gathered up a stack of books and at our usual time sat down to read. We had read several when we came to one that started with this question: When a farmer puts a seed into the ground, how does the seed know what plant to become?

That's a pretty good question for a three-year-old. We went on reading, but the question stuck with me. It's an innocent one with an answer that seems almost absurdly simple. A seed is a seed is a seed. No one has to tell it anything. You put it into the ground; later, out comes a plant.

Yet, as simple as it may seem, the question intrigues me partly for the parallels it suggests with human nature. Something in that little bit of life knows what's going on. A kernel of corn always grows a corn stalk; a bean always grows more beans. I know of not one instance when a corn stalk grew from a bean, or vice versa. The seed always knows.

Whatever is present in the seed to give it its identity, this one fact we know: The essence of the plant is in the seed. The potential is there, so we know better than to hope for roses if we have planted onions, no matter how fervently we cultivate, water, and weed the garden.

Here we have an acceptable handle to grasp some truth about ourselves. Plants grow from seeds, which hold in themselves both their potential quality and their identity. In much the same way, our life springs from a central core. Solomon speaks of a center of life where the mind and soul and will and affection of men are represented. For this unique spark of life, Solomon used the word "heart."

Just as a plant can become nothing other than its seed dictates, so our lives will only become an expression of what our heart holds. Our lives will come to reveal our heart, just as surely as the plant shows what sort of seed was put into the ground. We are molded from our environment, of course, but the forces active there only shape, not determine, our nature.

Using various imagery, Solomon emphasizes the centrality and importance of the heart.

> *As in water face reflects face, so the heart of man reflects man (27:19).*

Just as a clear pool reflects a man's visage, his heart is where you may find his true identity and nature. Solomon also says,

> *Watch over your heart with all diligence, for from it flow the springs of life (4:23).*

What we will grow into is already present in the character and content of our heart. The plant springs from the seed.

The analogy goes further. If we put a blighted and weak seed into the ground, we will get a scrawny plant, lacking in good fruit. In that case, the best remedy will not be to cut off its barren branches and try grafting on better ones because the essence will remain the same. At its root, it will still be the same sickly plant. Likewise, if our heart is blighted and bitter, if it is ugly and angry, we must not hope to correct the problem simply by lopping something off and patching on something better. The trouble lies in the seed. An angry heart will produce crooked and gnarled branches.

If we attempt to graft on better ones, the best we can hope for is a cosmetic improvement. At root, we will still be the same person, and our same bitter life will flow into the good we try to put on.

Like a seed, the heart is the root from which all else, even our life-code, grows. Our life-code will be the working plan—the system of values dictated by the condition of our heart. Thus, if we wish to adopt a new life-code, we must go to its source: We will need a new heart.

THE HEART'S ALTERNATIVES

The Healthy Seed

The Bible shows that a human heart may have only one of two natures. Either it may be fixed on God and His way or it may be fixed on itself. No other possibility exists.

In Proverbs, Solomon admonishes his audience to "incline their hearts" to God's way and to the teaching he offers about that way.

> *Make your ear attentive to wisdom, incline your heart to understanding (2:2).*
>
> *Wisdom will enter your heart, and knowledge will be pleasant to your soul (2:10).*
>
> *Let your heart keep my commandments (3:1).*
>
> *Let your heart hold fast my words (4:4).*
>
> *Write [my commandments] on the tablet of your heart (7:3).*
>
> *Do not let your heart turn aside (7:25).*
>
> *He who loves purity of heart and whose speech is gracious, the king is his friend (22:11).*
>
> *Listen, my son, and be wise, and direct your heart in the way (23:19).*
>
> *Give me your heart, my son, and let your eyes delight in my ways (23:26).*

Notice how in each of these verses Solomon encourages his listeners to do something with their hearts. He is making an appeal to the controlling center of their lives, so they may go beyond mere feeling and whim. He is not simply interested in giving them information but altering the seed of their being, so they may live their lives in new ways.

The only way for our hearts to be fixed upon God and His ways is for us to repent of our sinfulness, of our prideful clinging to our own ways, and to trust in the Lord to purify our hearts. What Solomon was urging his listeners to do may be done for us by the sovereign work of Christ. While speaking about newly made converts in the days following Christ's return to heaven, the apostle Peter said, "God, who knows the heart, bore witness to them, giving them the Holy Spirit, just as He also did to us; and He made no distinction between us and them, *cleansing their hearts by faith*" (Acts 15:8–9). Once we give our hearts to God and accept His cleansing, we are beginning to build a biblical life-code. Otherwise, our heart remains fixed on itself and can only bear bitter fruit.

The Sickly Seed

The better option open to us is for our heart to be inclined to God and His way. Conversely, the other option is for our heart to be inclined away from Him and toward itself. Rather than being open to God, all our faculties would be concentrated on our own way. The first kind of seed is the necessary prerequisite for a biblical life-code; the second leads to discord and fragmentation. If the human heart is not fixed on God, it inevitably produces evil.

As Solomon says, the man who is turned away from God is one "who with perversity in his heart devises evil continually" (6:14). God hates "a heart that devises wicked plans" (6:18). Solomon uses the harlot as an example because she is "cunning of heart" (7:10). Those who are "perverse in heart are an abomination to the Lord" (11:20).

In Proverbs, we often find the word "perversity" used to describe the heart of someone who is turned away from God. Instead of being fixed on good, the perverse heart is fixed on evil. Not being inclined to truth, it is susceptible to falsehood. Not being energized by God, it is impotent in the face of temptation. Though we would like to think we can be fixed on our own way and still be good people, that is a delusion. While it is perhaps too strong to say that no good can come from a heart following its own way, we can certainly say that no heart following its own way can be fundamentally good. Therefore, it will inevitably produce evil, discord, strife, and spiritual disease.

Let's remember the seed dictates the nature of the plant. If the seed is bad, the plant will be stunted. If the seed is good, the plant will be healthy.

Man's Natural Inclination

The Bible does not leave us guessing which of these two seeds is naturally ours. God not only shows us the two alternatives, He describes with frightening clarity just where we stand. The basic nature of our heart is not something that becomes fixed at a mythical age often called "the age of accountability" nor is it something gradually created in us. Every child of Adam comes into this world with his heart already pointed away from God as a part of his entry kit into the human race. This is why we are plagued with bad life-codes. Even newborn infants carry in them a seed already bitter and ugly. As that child grows, this orientation of his heart will show itself. The seed will become evident in the plant. Whatever else it may one day become, every human heart is first a perverse one, which does not love God but resents Him. It does not instinctively follow truth (though it may in time be taught to do so) but uses truth to serve its own ends. It does not love others unselfishly but looks after itself first and last.

Though these descriptions may seem unfairly harsh, they are true.

The primary way this basic nature shows itself—the primary hindrance to a biblical life-code—is the pride in our hearts. Pride is choosing for ourselves and thus against God, the essence of all sin. We never need to learn how to be wise in our own eyes. We must learn how to trust and obey God. Solomon warned against pride that prevents wisdom.

> *Do not be wise in your own eyes; Fear the Lord and turn away from evil (3:7).*
>
> *"Proud," "Haughty," "Scoffer," are his names who acts with insolent pride (21:24).*
>
> *He who trusts in his own heart is a fool, but he who walks wisely will be delivered (28:26).*

Because we are proud, we suffer. Having hearts bent toward ourselves, we force God to work against us, instead of for us. He must fight to pour His blessings into our lives until we open them to Him. We reject His healing, His mercy, and His instruction as invasions of our sovereignty. As a result, we go on in spiritual illness and ignorance. Finally, because God is both just and merciful, we must face His judgment if we will not open our hearts to Him. If we will not accept His blessing, we must accept His wrath.

And against this wrath, too, Solomon warns.

> *The Lord will tear down the house of the proud (15:25).*
>
> *Pride goes before destruction, and a haughty spirit before stumbling (16:18).*
>
> *A man's pride will bring him low (29:23).*

HOW GOD TRANSFORMS THE SEED

If I suffer as a result of something over which I have no control, isn't that unjust? If my heart is sickly from my conception and if that perversity produces in me pride with

133

all of its evils, isn't God punishing me for something that I can do nothing about?

Granted, it may look as though we are doomed both to a life of discord and to the wrath of God as a result of something we have no power to alter. And in one sense, that is true. We suffer today because of the actions of our father Adam. We have no power to alter either the circumstances or the seed in us when we come into this world. So, our life-codes are inevitably bad ones.

Nonetheless, though our heart has its basic nature in the human race, we may alter our basic nature. Our hearts may be changed! What the horticulturist cannot do for plants, God can do for human lives. All our lives God bends His great energy to one awesome task—He attempts to convince us to let Him remake us.

From experience and from the Word, we learn of three things that must happen for the Lord to transform the seed of our life, and thus, for us to learn the biblical life-code.

Accept the Scrutiny of the Divine Gardener

God will not change us as long as we remain aloof. If we do not present our hearts willingly before Him to be changed, He will not steal them from us. If, on the other hand, we come humbly (though fearfully), willing to let Him probe and to change what He finds, our hearts can become sources of health and energy.

Solomon intimates what God must do for this to happen.

> *All the ways of a man are clean in his own sight, but the Lord weighs the motives (16:2).*

We like to believe we are in the right. We barrel through life justifying and excusing ourselves, but God probes deeper. He is unswervingly honest and forces us to be so, too. He pinpoints the motives we have acted upon, the forces that have propelled and guided our choices. This is a necessary step if we are to have our hearts transformed.

Accept the Divine Gardener's Diagnosis

After we have submitted to the scrutiny of the Master, we must accept His diagnosis of our hearts. As He probes our depths, He shows us where the problems lie and lays them absolutely bare before us. From experience, I can say this is never pleasant. It is not easy to see our innermost thoughts when no covering remains for our self-love. Neither is it easy to accept the diagnosis of the Gardener when His fingers touch those things that seem to us most dear and most innocent.

But if we want new hearts, new life-codes, new lives, we must not only submit to His scrutiny, we must accept His analysis and prescription and lay aside all argument and defense. Before God, there exists no Moral Liberties Union to argue for "soul's rights." Before God, we stand without covering and without excuse to receive His judgment and, if we accept it, His healing.

Accept the Divine Gardener's Continuing Cultivation

The third step in being transformed is a daily response to the pruning, fertilizing, and in-grafting God does.

These three steps produce what the New Testament calls being "born again." From this first experience of God's grace, the transformation continues a lifetime of training as our life gains new direction and bears new fruit. All through life, we must continue to place ourselves at the disposal of the Gardener to be pruned and fertilized as the need arises.

Spiritual progress often begins in a sense of dissatisfaction, in a hunger for something more. When such yearnings arise and we feel a discontentment with things as they exist in us, it is a good time for new growth in Christ. If this study has shown areas where your own approach to life is inadequate, take stock. Have you taken the first step of placing your life before God to be changed? Have you repented of your prideful ways and accepted Jesus Christ as your personal Savior? If so, probe deeper. Are there areas of your life that have been withheld from the Gardener's cultivation? Are there cherished parts you have not allowed Him to prune?

God never slights an inquiring heart. In building biblical life-codes, the Holy Spirit must have complete freedom to look over our shoulder, to reaffirm what is good and to correct what is wrong. Both God's affirmation and God's correction can be exciting experiences.

WHEN WISDOM WINS

Until we see it happen, we may wonder whether God can really remake a life so completely that His grace shines out of every part. I will never forget watching God transform Bill.

Bill's wife and daughters came to our church long before he ever showed any interest. Leaving Dad to sleep or to go fishing, together they made their way to church each Sunday. Bill wasn't a bad man. He just had no interest in God, the church, or church people. His work and his play were more important. Occasionally, we would pray for him, but as the years slid by without any sign of his warming to us, Bill slid more and more into the background.

But God never forgot him. Beneath Bill's leathery exterior, God kept his heart soft. Almost imperceptibly, He was drawing him closer and closer until one day, when the door of his heart was left ajar for a moment, God sent home the shaft Bill couldn't shake loose. Through a gospel message on television, God showed him he was a sinner facing a hopeless eternity if he didn't repent and give his life to Christ.

I'll never forget hearing Bill, wiping the tears from

his eyes, tell how he dropped to his knees like a child and called on God to save him. The old, leathery factory worker who had no time for God is almost gone now. In his place is a man whose love for God shines out of eyes that twinkle with warmth and good humor. The man who cared more about fishing than about God now spends part of every week serving the church.

No, it wasn't easy when God started remaking Bill's life. The first thing he had to do was face his old friends because he couldn't do the same things he had once done. The lunchroom at Bill's factory had on its walls a collection of nude pinups. When God started rebuilding his life, He showed Bill how far those pinups were from a healthy attitude toward women and love. So Bill explained to his old buddies and to his union officials how he had changed and why he objected to the posters. He wasn't a vigilante or a crusader for moral issues. He was trying to live by the new life-code God was building in him.

As expected, Bill's old friends weren't exactly thrilled with the new Bill. Deeply offended, they did all they could to freeze him out of the factory. They shunned him, sabotaged his work, and even threw bottles at him, but Bill held steady. Easy? Far from it! He was becoming a new man, and the process wasn't all sunshine, roses, and congratulations.

One day a letter came from union headquarters. Bill was commended for his character and determination in standing up for what he believed. A little later, the posters came down, which only infuriated the other men even more. Bill experienced many days of lonesomeness, persecution, and even physical danger. All the while God was breaking down the old walls in his heart and putting in a new tender, loving spirit. As best he could, he responded to his attackers patiently and kindly. Little by little as his co-workers saw the new person emerging, the storm abated. Today Bill is one of the most trusted and well-liked employees at his factory. He is a living example of what happens when God remakes a man.

Can God make something new out of tough, broken, battered lives? Can God transform hearts that are full of bitterness and sorrow? Can He change a life-code that has been nurtured in the soil of worldliness? Yes! I know. I've watched Him do it.

· ● ● ● ·

Proverbs shows us wisdom. We have seen what happens when we try living without wisdom as well as some of the treasures wisdom offers. We have learned about friendship, about righteousness, about ways of using words, and about wealth. We have also seen that God can transform our hearts and thus our life-codes.

One piece of wisdom remains—wisdom for the long run. When you finish this study, you will be faced with the daily grind of life. What was there to be faced yesterday will still be there. Solomon knew about the rigors of the long run, so he left us a few words to help us finish it.

10. Wisdom for the Long Run

The Book of Proverbs has shown us wisdom as the best approach to life and refreshment and advice in God's Word. Solomon finishes Proverbs by offering us three pieces of wisdom to help us in the long run of life.

THE LONG RUN

Five of my most enjoyable years were spent going to school at Faith Academy, a school for missionary children set in the foothills that surround Manila in the Philippine Islands. There on top of a hill lies the campus, where many of us made our first really American friends. It wasn't unusual for us to have spent most of our lives tucked away with our parents in remote provinces with Filipino children for friends. While we enjoyed them and made fast friendships among them, there was something special about being with kids from our own country.

One of my fondest memories about Faith, though, is the special treat one teacher gave us. During seventh grade, we had a study hall almost the last period of the day and after spending hours indoors, we would have little patience left for school work. Study hall would be almost impossible. Out of the kindness of her heart, our teacher would allow us, if we wished, to run on the roads around the school, which were generally deserted. (Our school was the only place to speak of in a radius of several miles, except for a country club, which was quiet and well-fenced.) When we ran, we were expected to behave just as though we were training for the cross-country team.

This wasn't easy. To begin with, the temperature was usually between ninety and one hundred degrees, and the sun would beat down as only a tropical sun can. Then, there were the roads themselves. Very few of them were level so we ran up and down the sides of small mountains. Perhaps because it wasn't that easy, not many volunteered to trade the boredom of study hall for the heat of running.

I was one who did. I always loved the quietness, the solitude, the steady slap, slap, slap of my tennis shoes on the tarmac. As I ran, light winds would rustle faintly through the tall grass beside the road. I would trade study hall for the road any day, and gladly.

Among those of us who ran, a sort of hero's awe was reserved for anyone who could make it up the "gut-killer" without stopping. The "gut-killer" was a road, perhaps close to a mile long, that wound its way up the side of an impossibly steep hill. It was the test. This hill separated the stumblebums from the real runners. It was our dream, our highest aspiration, to run the gut-killer without stopping. If you stopped, you failed. If you turned around and went back down for an easier way, you failed miserably. You were no longer welcomed in the fraternity of runners.

The day came when I decided I was ready to face the hill. After warming up with an easy run by another route to the bottom of the hill, I screwed up my courage and started up. It was like running up stairs. Each step took more energy than the one before. The farther I ran, the harder it got to put one foot in front of the other. My wind gave out, my side hurt, my feet burned. But every time I thought of giving up, a little voice would whisper in my ear, *Try it a little farther. The top can't be far. Keep going. Just a little more. The top is closer now.*

I'll have to be honest. I can't remember if I actually *ran* all the way up. Although my pace got awfully slow from time to time, I do know one thing—I didn't stop! I made it to the top of the hill. I conquered the gut-killer!

Since those seventh-grade running days, I've often thought life is a lot like that hill. As we run, a long, solitary road stretches in front of us. We can usually only see the first hundred yards or so before it disappears tantalizingly round a bend. We have no idea what we will find. From rumors among the other runners, we hear the road is stocked with lots of hills and turns and drop-offs. But we keep on running. It's solitary because even though others run, too, theirs is another race. Each of us makes his own way. We can never deputize anyone else to run for us, though we may, from time to time, offer and receive aid. When we hit the hills, we sometimes wonder if we'll make it. At times we pass lovely scenery but often we face frightening circumstances. Yet we keep going.

Our future lies ahead. We are still engaged in our own private race, with our own private ogres still staring us in the face. So to help us face the long run, Solomon has these three rules to follow.

Running Requires Self-control

First, the long run requires self-control.

> Let your eyes look directly ahead, and let your gaze be fixed straight in front of you. Watch the path of your feet, and all your ways will be established (4:25–26).

Many things will distract us on the road. We may be tempted to stop and examine something we find along the way. Sometimes, we will be tempted to stop and rest at places we shouldn't. And of course, we ought always to enjoy the unfolding scenery of life. But we must never forget our goal. Life isn't just an aimless, purposeless drift through crazy circumstances. Our mind must continually be fixed on the road ahead. Rather than simply moving with the winds, we need to exercise control over our spirit to keep our lives pointed aright.

Like a city that is broken into and without walls is a man who has no control over his spirit (25:28).

There will come times when we will have to say to ourselves, *Yes I know that looks like an appealing thing to do (choice to make, feeling to have, place to go, idea to follow), but the Bible tells me what I ought to do, so I will do it.* Here's the function of self-control in the long run.

Running Requires Contentment

The long run requires a curious blend between a desire to keep going and a contentment with life as it is. This is Solomon's second piece of advice: If we slip completely to one or the other of these extremes, we encounter difficulty. We must not be complacent. We must always keep the horizon in view, yet we must run the present race to its fullest, not slighting the present for some dangling lure in the future.

Solomon recognized two sources of nourishment for those who run. Joy is one; contentment, the other. A broken spirit soon breaks down all our faculties, but a joyful spirit spreads refreshment through all our life. Likewise, a passionate, restless discontentment with life saps our strength, while an acceptance and joy in the living of life is a constant source of stamina.

A joyful heart is good medicine, but a broken spirit dries the bones (17:22).

Wisdom is in the presence of the one who has understanding, but the eyes of the fool are on the ends of the earth (17:24).

How often we strain at our tethers, craning our necks to reach the grass of another pasture, searching for wisdom down another lane when peace and satisfaction lie at our feet! We need to learn to balance a healthy regard for what lies round the next turn with a contentment in running the present stretch of road.

Running Requires Hope

Solomon's third piece of advice for the long run is that life demands hope. No hill is too long, no ford too swift, no track too narrow. We can make it through! Listen again to Solomon.

> *The hope of the righteous is gladness, but the expectation of the wicked perishes (10:28).*

Sometimes things look pretty hopeless. We struggle from time to time with problems that seem to defy solution. Marriage tensions, family crises, career failures look as though they will defeat us. For the righteous—for those who learn wisdom—gladness may spring up even in the face of such challenges. Like a fresh spring throwing its spray down the mountain, God's hope showers our lives and sends flowers where we least expect them. There is always hope!

If it is to come from us, hope will certainly fail. We are not strong enough. Our resources are too slim. What we must remember is that our resources are only the first hints of His, our strength merely a suggestion of His. Our hope rests in our Father. This is one of Proverbs' most encouraging messages: God not only fills us with His wisdom but stands ready to fight our battles with us, and nothing can defeat Him.

> *There is no wisdom and no understanding and no counsel against the Lord. The horse is prepared for the day of battle, but victory belongs to the Lord (21:30–31).*

This is wisdom for the long run. On this, our life-codes must be built.

> *Do not let your heart envy sinners, but live in the fear of the Lord always. Surely there is a future, and your hope will not be cut off. Listen, my son, and be wise, and direct your heart in the way (23:17–19).*

THE LAST WORD

Because I had seen in Proverbs a particular way of life that seemed worthy of special treatment, I have written this book. Wisdom was, for Solomon, how he knew life ought to be lived. Wisdom is, at core, a living relationship with God from which are born all the treasures we have attempted to share here.

Perhaps the most beautiful product of that living relationship is the enduring hope it bears in the hearts of those who share it.

Life is not overlong for the healthiest of us. Neither is it without its rigors. Without the intimate relationship with God that is the source of wisdom, life too often degenerates into a messy affair. And yet, as I look about, I find in the lives of those who live by wisdom a freshness and a vision that is appealing.

The message of this book is that life does not have to be discordant, but harmonious. A full and useful life may be ours and beyond it, the hope of an even greater glory than we can now conceive. We were not meant for despair. Hope is the inheritance Christ left for the human race. Hope may be ours!

I would like to leave you with the story of a young man whose life came to radiate wisdom.

Rufino's father was a member of a head-hunting tribe whose village was tucked far back in the high mountains of northern Luzon. All his life he had followed the ways of his ancestors, farming, fighting as the need arose, keeping his obligation to the spirits by animal and grain sacrifices. He was a short man, not five feet tall. He wore a dirty loincloth, and an old coat warded off the cool of the mountain air. His deep brown skin was seamed and leathered by the rain and the wind and the smoke of countless fires. The hard lines of his face mirrored the hardness of his life, and the expression in his eyes was one of resignation, fear, yet smoldering pride.

He was getting on in years when my father found his way back through the hills and into his village. Dad went with a Filipino pastor to share the word of Jesus Christ among the mountain tribes. When they came to this village, they stopped and talked to those who would listen. Squatting on the ground, Rufino's father listened to my father and the pastor stoically as they gave the message of God, who made Himself a man to take on Himself the sins of man and thus to die for them.

The story moved Rufino's father. But the hold of the years was too strong on him, and he said to my father, "Your story is a good one and though you have come too late for me, in our village are many young people. I would like for you to tell them the story so they can know this God of yours who can free them from the spirits."

In that village lived Rufino, short like his father, but with a life to be lived still before him. My father did preach to the young people. Rufino weighed the ways of his ancestors and read there the years of fear and bondage and hatred, but he heard in the story a way out—a way he could not refuse. On his ancestors' mountain, Rufino took a new step. Breaking with the past, he placed his heart and life in the hands of Christ to be made new.

The years that followed were full ones.

Before long, Rufino left his mountains and went to the lowlands to the Bible school, where he could learn more about his faith and train to be a pastor to his people. By western standards, Rufino was not much to boast of. He had little education and even less knowledge of life outside his mountains. He would not buy a large tube of toothpaste because he knew it would spoil before he could use all of it.

English was the national language of the Philippines. Since Rufino did not know much English, he spent many an afternoon, while his fellows rested, on his knees with his Bible open before him and a dictionary open beside it. He would read a few lines, stop to consult his dictionary, then pray and cry before the Lord, almost in despair of ever understanding or getting back to his mountains. By most anyone's standards, Rufino wasn't the one most likely to succeed.

But God was with Rufino. His natural stubbornness and his determination to finish eventually won out. He graduated from school and with a song in his heart, headed back toward the mountains to preach about a way of life that set men free from the fear of the spirits and gave them a future. The last time I saw Rufino, we shared a meal together in his home, perched high above the mountain city where he had been assigned with others to plant a new church.

In Rufino and his father, I have seen, unforgettably, what God can do in a life yielded to Him. While Rufino's father lay dying, a shaman held a live chicken over his head and plucked out its feathers in hopes that the noise would drive away the evil spirits. It was an ugly end to a hard and hopeless life.

But from Rufino's eyes shine a merry spirit and a certainty that life is full of hope. His face has none of the hardness of his father's, but the traces of a life lived with purpose and meaning. Rufino is living proof of the difference made when a life is lived for God.

I know that from Cincinnati to San Diego, from Newark to Nashville are people wrestling with lives full of hurt and sorrow and anger. They are in bondage to the wrong choices of the past. In place of joy, there is pain; in place of hope, despair.

I know, as well, that these lives may be made new. The choice of life-codes can be made any day. To those who are struggling, I give Wisdom's invitation.

Turn to my reproof, behold, I will pour out my spirit on you; I will make my words known to you (1:23).

He who listens to me shall live securely, And shall be at ease (1:33).

These words are true. I know. Ready to try them?

NOTES

CHAPTER 1.

1. *New American Standard Bible,* (Chicago: Moody Press, 1975). Hereafter, unless otherwise noted in the body of the text, all references to the Bible are taken from this translation.

2. Franz Delitzsch, ed., *Biblical Commentary on the Proverbs of Solomon,* Vol. I (Grand Rapids: Wm. B. Eerdmans Publishing Co., 1968), p. 54.

3. Delitzsch, Vol. I. I am indebted to the discussion of the wisdom literature here in which the writer suggests that a basic grasp of reality is inherent in the Hebrew concept of wisdom.

4. Delitzsch, Vol. I, p. 54. The idea that Wisdom gives one the ability to discern the true from the false, the valuable from the valueless receives treatment here.

5. Delitzsch, Vol. I, p. 56.

CHAPTER 2.

1. Delitzsch, Vol. I, p. 55.

2. *Webster's Seventh New Collegiate Dictionary,* definition of "rote."

3. Charles T. Fritch, Rolland W. Schloerb, George A. Buttrick, eds., *The Interpreter's Bible,* Vol. IV (New York: Abingdon Press, 1952), p. 778.

4. Delitzsch, Vol. I, p. 58.

5. *The Holy Bible, New International Version* (Grand Rapids: Zondervan Bible Publishers, 1978).

CHAPTER 3.

1. The imagery of old men sitting on their park benches comes from Paul Simon.
2. Delitzsch, Vol. I, p. 69.
3. Delitzsch, Vol I, p. 69.

CHAPTER 4.

1. Delitzsch, Vol. I, p. 69.
2. D. Guthrie, J. A. Motyer, eds., *The New Bible Commentary, Revised* (Grand Rapids: Wm. B. Eerdmans Publishing Co., 1970), p. 533.
3. Delitzsch, Vol I, p. 85.
4. Delitzsch, Vol I, p. 87.
5. Delitzsch, Vol I, p. 88.

CHAPTER 5.

1. George MacDonald, edited by Michael Phillips, *The Fisherman's Lady* (Minneapolis: Bethany House Publishers, 1982), pp. 259–60.
2. MacDonald, pp. 262–63.
3. Used by permission, Singspiration, 1948.

CHAPTER 6.

1. H. A. Ironside, *Proverbs* (Neptune: Loizeaux Brothers, 1908), p. 388.
2. Delitzsch, Vol. II, pp. 213–14.

CHAPTER 7.

1. Carl F. H. Henry, ed., *The Biblical Expositor* (Philadelphia: A. J. Holman Co., 1973), p. 465.

2. Henry, p. 471.
3. Henry, p. 471.

CHAPTER 8

1. Delitzsch, Vol. I, p. 265.
2. Delitzsch, Vol. II, pp. 161–62.